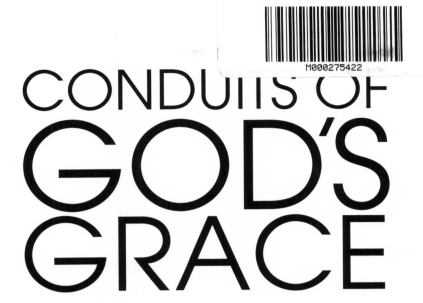

CONDUITS OF
GOD'S
GRACE

Books by Merrill J. Oster

Professional Hedging Handbook, 1974

Practical Principles of Gathering, 1976

Commodity Futures for Profit ... A Farmer's Guide to Hedging, 1979

Multiply Your Money Trading Soybeans, 1981

Farmland Buying Strategies, 1984

How to Multiply Your Money: A Beginner's Guide to Futures/Options Trading, 1986

Father to Son: Becoming a Man of Honor, 1988

Vision-Driven Leadership, 1991

Becoming a Woman of Purpose: Father to Daughter, 1993

The Osters in America, 1994

The Entrepreneur's Creed: The Principles & Passions of 20 Successful Entrepreneurs, 2001

Giving Back: Using Your Influence to Create Social Change, 2003

You Can Change the World, 2012

CONDUITS OF GOD'S GRACE

92 Life Tips from the Founder of
Pinnacle Forum and 20 Startups

Merrill J. Oster

PINNACLE FORUM
TRANSFORMING LEADERS
TO TRANSFORM CULTURE

PINNACLE FORUM
TRANSFORMING LEADERS
TO TRANSFORM CULTURE

Published by Pinnacle Forum
7950 E. Acoma Drive Suite 211 Scottsdale, AZ 85260
480-609-7000
https://pinnacleforum.com

First printing — April 2019

Cover design: Steve Welter, 1Vision
Interior design: Lisa Barnes, Niddy Griddy Design, Inc.

Dedication

To Carol, the love of my life for her patience through 57 years of marriage and counting.

To the memory of my brother, Larry, who passed from this life into the next while I was writing this book.

To my mentors, the conduits of God's grace through whom I have been blessed in so many ways. Also to my coworkers who were co-mentors on teams of peers who built financial information service companies that impacted hundreds of thousands of members, clients and customers.

Contents

Acknowledgments

Thanks to my friend Mike Hamel who turned on his recorder, transcribed hours of my ramblings, edited out the minutiae, then arranged my words and memories into an orderly fashion. His patience through my seven draft rewrites and encouragement to launch this project in the first place are gratefully appreciated.

Thanks also to my peers whom Mike interviewed for Chapter 12. Their time and perspective on our history revived memories that helped me piece together our wonderful story. And to my wife, Carol, who put up with many eight-hour days when the process of digging into my memories put me in my own little world for long periods.

"Honey, I'm back!"

Foreword

In *Conduits of God's Grace*, Merrill Oster gives us 92 life tips that are potential life changers. I know his advice works because after working for Merrill, he was the mentor who most encouraged me to take a risk and buy my own company when other advisers thought the deal was too risky. Then, as a board member, he spelled out five business changes that turned my company around to profitability and an IPO several years later.

Merrill's wise and caring advice changed the trajectory of my life and equipped me to become a businessman scaling ministries that serve people through combining the Great Commission with the Great Commandment. His investment of his time and talent led me to invest in my company's team and, later, in the investors, employees and clients of Opportunity International and Edify.org, a ministry I started to improve and expand sustainable Christ-centered education for children living in poverty globally. In these far off places, new conduits of God's grace are being formed as one person influences another in their walk with the Lord.

I hope this book helps you see your role as a conduit of God's grace to those around you as together we build God's kingdom.

Christopher A. Crane,
former CEO of COMPS InfoSystems,
Opportunity International and Edify.org

Introduction
Why Now?

Carol, my wife of 57 years, has been nudging me to write my (our) life story for years. Mike Hamel, a coauthor on a few earlier books, became a bit of a nag about getting an autobiography in print. So why now?

A few months ago, I turned 78. I decided to get an opinion on how much time I had left, so I spoke to my iPhone, "Hey, Siri, how long will I live?" In a very unemotional tone, she replied, "The average American male has a life span of seventy-eight years."

That response set things in motion!

Always seeking a second opinion, I Googled the life expectancy of a 78-year-old male. Answer: "If you make it to 78, statistics show you have 9.17 more years." That response took a little pressure off.

I breathed a sigh of relief, called Mike and told him to turn on his recorder because I was about to dump a series of downloads on him in hopes he could make sense of it all and do so before the end of my journey.

By the grace of God, after many drafts, here we are.

I am approaching my 79th birthday as I write this book. Looking back, it's a bit easier to see the evidence of God at work lavishing favor (grace) on me in so many ways. Today I see more clearly than ever before the powerful work of the Holy Spirit quietly influencing my life through so many wonderful people. My mentors. My influencers. My peers. My coworkers.

This is the story of how God used these powerful influencers as conduits of his love to nudge me from one stage in life to the next and to provide insights on one decision after another. They were conduits of his grace.

Some of them, like my parents and grandparents, spent decades shaping me. Some labored beside me for years. Others had a brief but significant impact; a moment in time when a single sentence by a mentor delivered an insight that was just what was needed. With their help, I went from an Iowa farm boy soaking up life tips from family to becoming an entrepreneur starting, acquiring and leading 25 financial service, real estate and agribusiness companies with 275,000 customers and 400 employees in 16 countries.

This book pays tribute to these unconventional and often unknowing heroes who influenced me, including family, friends, teachers, mentors, employers and peers. At every key crossroad, God sent someone to give needed guidance just as he promises his disciples in John 14:26. "But the Advocate, the Holy Spirit, whom the Father will send in my name, will teach you all things and will remind you of everything I have said to you." God has spoken to me many times through his Bible, through the nudges from the Holy Spirit and frequently through another of his servants working alongside.

In these pages I reflect on both the large and the seemingly small things folks did to shine a light on my path. This book is my tribute to them, and my public thanksgiving to God who transmitted his truth to me through them and through his Word. This book is also about some of the people God has allowed me to influence. They are men and women who have gone on to accelerate change in their families, communities, the nation and the world. This isn't an exaggeration, as you will see in the pages that follow. I am thrilled and amazed and humbled by them and what they are accomplishing!

I hope *Conduits of God's Grace* inspires you to look back and see yourself as a recipient of insight and grace from God at critical times as others have shined their light on your path. And I hope this book encourages you to look around for opportunities to be a conduit of God's grace to others. In the end, the goal of mankind is to love God and serve others. The best way to do that is to be a channel of his love and grace.

Business Overview
Oster Communications, Inc.

In 1969, after nearly seven years working for John Strohm Associates in Woodstock, Illinois, I returned home to Cedar Falls, Iowa, to launch Communication Consultants (ComCo), a marketing advisory firm with many agribusiness clients. It became the base for a financial publishing firm with a global reach. In 1973 my longtime friend and mentor, Jerry Carlson, left his managing editor role at *Farm Journal* to partner with me in starting Professional Farmers of America. Jerry's outstanding editorial skills positioned the *Pro Farmer* newsletter to become an immediate and stunning success.

Our "starting five" leadership team consisted of Jerry, Darrell Jobman, Rex Wilmore, Larry Graham and Mike Walsten. I was their player-coach. Our group changed how farmers saw themselves: as professionals. The team created new types of financial analysis and marketing advice based on the use of commodity futures. We dramatically reshaped how information was delivered: from first-class mail newsletter to real-time satellite and internet. We leveled the playing field between farmers and the huge grain corporations by teaching Pro Farmer members how to use futures markets to manage risk.

Pro Farmer Institute attracted thousands of its 30,000 Professional Farmers of America members to training seminars on futures marketing, land buying and other profit-making and risk-management topics.

In 1976, we acquired *Commodities* magazine with 3,000 subscribers and grew it into *Futures* magazine with 65,000 subscribers. *Futures* became the most highly regarded publication in the world's fast-growing commodity and financial futures markets. Its Commodity Price Charts and Investor Publications were industry leaders. The Commodity

Education Institute trained hundreds of aspiring traders and brokers.

The 1981 acquisition of Commodity Communications Corp. positioned Oster Communications to receive real-time price information from every futures exchange in the world. With the founding of *Futures World News* (and its successor Oster Dow Jones Commodity News) and the development of proprietary software, the company became FutureSource and FutureSource UK.

Oster Communications formed three service companies to meet our internal needs: Parkade Properties bought and renovated 100,000 square feet of office space, stimulating a dramatic rebirth of Main Street in Cedar Falls. Teledirect was our direct marketing division. American Graphics Services provided prepress functions for our many publications and many outside clients.

The Oster companies assembled 400 business associates with offices in 16 countries. We served 275,000 financial decision makers in 32 countries from the original base in Cedar Falls, Iowa, where we also published the *Cedar Falls Citizen* newspaper and the *HomeTowner* shopper. We launched 30 or more unique brands and rolled them into six companies that were dressed for sale as opportunities and threats emerged in the marketplace.

Oster companies today include Pinnacle Prairie, a 720-acre real estate development in Cedar Falls, and Oster Partners, a real estate investment firm with properties in Iowa, Wisconsin, Illinois and Arizona.

I have also been blessed to have been the founder of Pinnacle Forum, a leadership organization aimed at encouraging a wave of cultural influencers to invest their lives in executing cultural change strategies that change lives and make this a better world through Christian service.

Oster Comunications

Comco Clients
- American Soybean Assn
- Amchem
- Hubbard Milling
- Central National Bank
- Elanco
- American Bank Newsletter
- Top Farmers of America
- Banking Magazine
- Agrifinance Magazine
- Successful Farming Magazine
- Chicago Open Board of Trade

Professional Farmers of America
- Pro Farmer Newsletter
- Corn Pro
- Pork Pro
- Landowner
- ProFarmer Institute
- Management Monthly
- Pro Playback
- Globalink

FutureSource
- FutureSource UK
- Futurelink

Futures Magazine
- Commodity Price Charts
- Commodity Education Institute
- Investor Publications
- Corporate Risk Management
- Commodities Report
- TraderSource
- Capitalist Edge
- Futures Learning Center
- Futures International Conferences

Futures World News
- Oster Dow Jones Commodity News

American Graphics Services

Other Oster Companies
- Teledirect
- Parkade Properties
- Pinnacle Prairie
- Oster Farms
- Oster Pork
- Commodity Hedgers and Traders
- Hometowner/Citizen
- Oster Partners
- Naperville Magazine

One

Farm Boy
From the Barnyard toward the Boardroom

You have parents and grandparents who have spectacular reputations in this community. You've got big shoes to fill.
— Pearl Oster

The winds of World War II were whipping around the world on May 30, 1940, the day I was born. The Oster family had survived the Great Depression, but the scars of sacrifice were deep. Then a new global event, Pearl Harbor, was about to hit our Iowa farming community on December 7, 1941.

My first memories of life were happy faces and loving hugs inside the house, shades pulled in case invading aircraft might spot and target our town, Cedar Falls, and people speaking in hushed tones to protect little ones like me from hearing the harsh realities of wartime life.

I'm an Iowa farm boy with a wonderful heritage. I've always felt I was born rich. Not that the Osters had much money. But I had a wealth of rich relationships and loving people teaching me vital life tips, starting with my grandparents and parents. I grew up on a farm situated in Grundy County between Cedar Falls and New Hartford, Iowa. We raised corn, soybeans, hay, hogs, cattle and chickens.

Dad rented 240 acres on the northeast corner of the intersection of County Road X and what was then US Highway 20, a ribbon of concrete that crosses America from coast to coast. The house, chicken house and outhouse were on one side of the dirt road; the barn, hog house and corn crib on the other. The two-story, four-bedroom house had running water and electricity but neither hot water nor indoor bathroom. It was heated by a basement furnace hand fed with corncobs left by the shellers, wood chopped from the grove of trees and coal delivered from the Cedar Falls Coal Company. Larry (my brother) and I rejoiced when the owner finally installed a bathroom and stoker furnace.

The living room was right above the furnace, so it got nice and warm, whereas my upstairs bedroom was pretty cold on winter mornings. The family gathered around the open heat register early in the morning while the house warmed up. The radio was constantly spouting out the news. The radio and the newspapers and the magazines fueled our conversation around that heat register and the breakfast table.

In the evenings after chores, we gathered in the living room where the big radio stood. It must have been four feet tall. We listened to programs like Gene Autry and The Lone Ranger while playing board games. The radio pulled in local stations KWWL and KXEL in Waterloo as well as WMT in Cedar Rapids and WHO in Des Moines. On a clear night, we would pull in WGN in Chicago.

Radio wasn't just entertainment; we lived on news. World news had an impact on me even as a child. I saw my mother weep as she ran across the yard to tell Dad that President Roosevelt had passed on April 12, 1945. I saw the concern in Dad's eyes as he talked about the opening of the Korean War in June 1950 with the man behind the counter at the International Harvester implement dealership in Cedar Falls. I watched Mom and Dad sit soberly listening to every word of McArthur's famous retirement speech on April 19, 1951.

My parents' interest in the news probably sparked my interest in journalism. A big part of my business career would be providing relevant, market-moving news to farmers and commodity traders around the world. The farm broadcaster I remember listening to in my living room in the 1950s, Dallas McGinnis, would later hire and mentor me as a broadcaster when I went to college in 1958. From 1959 to 1961, I was a regular on WOI radio and an occasional broadcaster on WOI TV in Ames, Iowa. But I'm getting ahead of myself.

My paternal grandparents, Jim and Bessie Oster, farmed just across Highway 20 until I was 12. When Grandpa Jim retired from farming in 1953, Dad purchased 80 acres of the farm that had been in the Oster family since great-grandparents Knud and Marie had planted the Osters on it in 1898. They had bought 160 acres from the original homesteader for $40 an acre in 1898. Grandpa Jim and Aunt Julia Crose inherited the farm but lost half of it during the Great Depression. My parents bought the 80 acres with the buildings and eventually were able to retrieve the other 80 acres to bring the original 160-acre farmstead back into the family at a price of $400 per acre in 1953. My land buying story comes later, but note, that's a tenfold increase in land prices in 55 years. The next tenfold increase came between 1953 and 1990—just 37 years!

The Osters were devout Christians. That means they constantly lived out what they believed. Grandpa Jim was a Sunday School teacher in the Methodist Church. When the church went liberal, he moved the family to the Walnut Street Baptist Church in Waterloo. These were still horse-

and-buggy days, making the eight-mile trip to Waterloo a significant sacrifice and show of commitment to their faith. **Life tip #1: Stand on the Word of God.**

Grandpa Jim had a gruff exterior but was a tenderhearted guy underneath. His outer edge never frightened me because I always saw the twinkle in his eyes and his loving side. He loved to tease and make jokes. I've inherited his ability to give the tough things in life a humorous spin. He loved having kids around and took an interest in the grandkids from the time we were small. He hid candy peanuts and Life Savers under the front seat, then pretended to be mad at the kids who swiped them. I drove his old Jeep when I was only six and later drove his tractors well before my dad thought I was ready. Sometimes he would pull into our yard and call out, "I'm going to town. Can Merrill come along?" That was music to my ears! I was otherwise trapped on the farm. This was my ticket to go see what was happening in Cedar Falls.

My Grandma Bessie was as soft-spoken as Grandpa was outspoken. She was a regular Bible reader, a faithful church-goer and a real prayer warrior. She bought my first Bible and took me to Sunday School at Walnut Street Baptist Church in Waterloo. Grandma Bessie tended a large garden, cared for a flock of chickens and somehow managed to keep the house clean and the family fed despite having neither running water nor modern appliances in the house. She put God first in her life. She loved to tell of her "marvelous conversion."
Life tip #2: Put God first.

When Grandpa and Grandma Oster retired from farming and moved to Cedar Falls in 1953, Grandpa expanded the saw and disc sharpening business he had started while still running the farm. He was a colorful guy. He got by driving a 1950 Chevy he bought for $50, then he hand-painted it yellow! He knew how to live modestly, making his Social Security check stretch from one month to the next. When I offered to help him financially, he replied, "Heck, no. Ma and I have everything we need."

Grandpa Jim died in 1975 at age 89, just two weeks after he asked me to be his "manager." That was his way of asking me to look out for Grandma after he passed. Grandma Bessie died 10 years later at 93.

My maternal grandparents, Fred and Carrie Smith, lived close by in Benson, Iowa. They had been won to Christ in 1922 by evangelist Oliver Smith—no relation. They went on to help start Stout Gospel Hall in Stout, Iowa, that I also attended as a child. Grandpa Fred was a kind, intelligent man who took a special interest in me and my brother, Larry. He and Grandma frequently looked after us when Dad and Mom needed a night out.

Grandpa farmed near Dike, then worked as a teletype operator for the railroad. He began to lose his mental skills as a result of a brain tumor, probably from an injury while operating a road grader for Butler County when he was hit in the head by a rock. He passed away at age 60 in 1948 when I was only eight. I was blessed to have logged a lot of hours with him before then: sitting in his lap in the kitchen, walking into the field with him to get the cows. His was the first death close to me and an absolute heartbreaker. It also got my dad's attention.

Life tip #3: Love one another by investing quality time.

Dad grew up in a Christian home but had never made a profession of faith. His father-in-law's death triggered him to think about eternity. Shortly after Grandpa died, Dad accepted the Lord late in 1948. He began to witness to me from time to time in a gentle, loving way. He would pick me up, walk up the steep stairs, tuck me into bed and say something like, "Merrill, someday you're going to have to make the same decision I have. You must keep thinking about these eternal things."

After Grandpa Fred died, Grandma Carrie couldn't afford to maintain her home. So, she moved in with us and became a second mother to Larry and me from the time I was nine until I left for college. I got to see my mother's impact on my grandmother and vice versa. They had a wonderful relationship and deep respect for one another.

Grandma Carrie became the keeper of the house when my mom restarted her school-teaching career. Grandma was also a keeper of the peace between us boys. Larry and I had a way of getting into each other's hair. She settled a good many disputes with a few well-chosen words. At other times she kept us out of trouble with Dad, warning us of his wrath to come. "Your dad isn't very happy with the way you cleaned the separator room. If I were you, I'd get down there and clean it up right before you get a licking." We would hightail it out the door to correct our sloppiness.

Grandma Carrie was a consistent witness for Christ and known for her enthusiasm to see others find a right relationship with the Lord. She sat on the edge of our bed and explained to Larry and me that we were sinners who needed to accept Jesus Christ as our Savior. I was probably five or six at the time. She walked the talk, and Larry and I knew it. Others did also. Folks from all around stopped at the house for Grandma's counsel, prayer and cookies. She integrated her faith into every area of life. Her conversation could go from cookies to the Cross and back to cookies so smoothly that talking about Jesus seemed the most natural thing. No one other than my parents shaped my worldview and value system more than her. Not only did she lead me and Larry to the Lord as I relate in the next chapter, but she gave me my first lessons in discipleship and remained a constant source of love, instruction and encouragement. She made the best cinnamon rolls and pull-aparts in the county and attracted quite a following of friends who enjoyed her food and fellowship.

Life tip #4: Get a life — a spiritual one.

Grandma Carrie reached the ripe old age of 96. At her funeral I had the privilege of sharing the profound impact she had on so many people, including me. I later learned that she'd collected every bit of publicity about me that existed from my high school and college years. But somehow she forgot about the value of our baseball card collection and gave it to some lucky kid while Larry and I were in college. She continued to pour into my life after I left home, dropping what she was doing to visit me and Carol for a week or more to help with whatever was going on in our Woodstock, Illinois, home. Our children, David and Leah, got to benefit in some of the same ways I had from her loving presence.

Fred and Carrie's only child was my mother, Pearl. She was born prematurely in 1917. The doctor's wife had to care for her by placing her in an open oven on low heat during the first several weeks. Her parents became Christians in 1922 when she was only five. A few years after that, she also accepted Christ as her Savior after pondering Ephesians 2:8–9: "For it is by grace you have been saved, through faith — and this is not from yourselves, it is the gift of God — not by works, so that no one can boast."

Mom grew up to become a teacher and taught all eight grades in one-room rural schools in Grundy, Black Hawk and Butler Counties. The schools had neither running water nor automatic heat, so she shoveled coal in the mornings before the kids got there and made sure their coats were on when they went to the outhouse.

For a brief time my mother was my teacher at the Fairfield No. 3 school near our home. It didn't have indoor plumbing until I was in the seventh grade. We never did get running water. The older boys ran up to the Oster farm for that. The school was called the Oster School because my father, grandfather and great-grandfather had been members of the board and school board presidents who volunteered to shovel snow, mow grass and do general maintenance. They wrote the checks for the teachers and sometimes kept them in their homes.

In that one-room rural elementary school, the faster-learning older kids helped the younger. The teacher would ask the older kids like me to monitor the reading class of the younger ones. Then she would have us sit down with a fourth grader and help him with math. I was getting some early training as a teacher.

One day as a first grader, I got in a fight with an eighth grader who called my Mom an "old bag." I attacked the big guy with my fists and got my clock cleaned. Mom decided that defending her honor was a burden I was too young to carry. She sent me to the New Hartford School for the rest of that year. The next year we traded places. She went to work for New Hartford Consolidated Schools. I returned to the one-room schoolhouse. She taught first and second grades for 28 years before retiring in 1980. She taught more than 1,000 kids how to read. Her dedication to her students was legendary. She loved her work and she loved kids, both her own kids and her school kids.

• • •

Even as a child I could pick up that the Great Depression had a huge impact on my mother, more so than it did my father. She walked the railroad tracks picking up spilled coal to save a little money for the family. She received a pair of socks at Christmas 1934, and then, realizing her parents didn't have the money, she returned them and brought the money back home. I became very economically sensitive as a result of this depression-driven frugality of my mother. It wasn't just my parents, but my friends' parents were also always looking for ways to save a dime. "A penny saved is a penny earned" was an expression that meant something in the 1940s when five pennies would buy a cup of coffee or a sack of candy large enough to give a kid a bellyache.

To maintain her teaching credentials, Mom took summer school classes at Iowa State Teacher's College (now the University of Northern Iowa). While at the library she checked out books for me to read. I was an avid reader and would go through several during the summers. She taught Larry and me that our parents and grandparents had earned good reputations in Cedar Falls and New Hartford. Upholding our family reputation through good behavior and helping others were topics of our regular dinner table conversation.

Mom died in 1994, just a few months after Grandma Carrie's death. I wrote a tribute to Mom shortly before and presented it to her publicly as part of the 25th anniversary of Oster Communications. It was fitting because she planted so many good things in my life that showed up in the corporate culture of our companies and in the community work I did. It captures just a fraction of all I'm thankful for:

You watched me like an "old setting hen" as Dad would say, then at just the right time you set me free. Free to come and go. To decide which 4-H projects to take on. To decide how to spend my free time. You gave me great memories . . . driving across the state to a speech contest or essay contest, being in my cheering section when I played ball, gave a speech or showed a 4-H pig or calf. You never left me unprotected. You didn't leave home to teach school until Grandma could step in to help out. . . . You loved my Dad and together made a good home.

In one of her last public events, Mom was in the audience when the Regent Theatre celebrated its new grand opening in 1994. Carol and I made a naming-level gift, and as a result, the theatre became known as the Oster Regent Theatre in honor of her and Dad.

Life tip #5: Protect your reputation.

My dad, Harland James Oster, was a man of many talents. Despite the loss of an eye at age four, he adapted well enough to help his New Hartford high school basketball team make it to the state tournament in 1936. He was a crack shot with either a basketball or a gun. He could drop a pheasant or duck from 50 yards. Even as a boy he put in 12-hour days on the farm, tackling the toughest jobs with a steady pace. He grew up on the Oster home place, worked on neighboring farms, then went to work at Benson Creamery before renting his first farm. In 1942 he rented 240 acres from owners Charles Struntze and later, Hans Christofferson. He farmed there until he saved enough money to buy 80 acres, half of the original home farm, from his dad in 1953.

Dad was a well-respected farmer, good businessman and great teacher. I have fond memories of him putting me on his lap on a tractor so I could ride along. When I was 10, he bought a small tractor, a Farmall C, so I could plow a field working beside or behind him on his Farmall M. That allowed me to be in the field for hours and hours with Dad as a peer.

I loved working alongside Dad. He taught me life tips in practical ways. I was six years old when I got the task of filling the tank in the hog house. I forgot to turn the water off a time or two and flooded the place, for which I got disciplined. (That meant being spanked with a whip!) Then, after the tears were wiped away, Dad handed me a scoop shovel and helped clean up the mess I had created. I began to understand the cause-and-effect relationship between failure to follow directions and negative outcomes. He had a soft demeanor and liked to tease, but he wasn't afraid to scold in a loud voice or use a switch to correct repeated wrongdoings.

Life tip #6: Bad decisions have bad consequences.

I received training and verbal approval from Dad for what I was doing. I would be tagging along with him, and he might say, "Here, Merrill. I've got to fill this burlap bag with corn. Would you hold it open for me?" As I did so, he explained how I was increasing the speed with which he could fill that bag and that without me it would take twice as long. "Son, you're doing a man's job." And I began to understand that I could play a significant role on the farm at a fairly early age.

Dad didn't try to pound common sense into me. He didn't push it at me; he just lovingly massaged me with it. One time we were shoveling corn into a wagon, and I was going at it with great vigor trying to get the job done fast. "Slow down, son," Dad said. "We got a full day's work ahead; you've got to learn to pace yourself."

Life tip #7: Pace yourself.

Then he added, "While you're pacing yourself on this boring job, let your mind think about the next two or three

things you have to do. Figure out what's going to be the next one and where you have to go so you don't waste a lot of steps in between."
Life tip #8: Have a plan.

Dad would tell me, "Decide what's most important and get those big jobs done first." Dad's lessons of pacing myself, setting priorities and planning the next step came into play in starting and running many companies.
Life tip #9: Set priorities.

My dad's early training on economics was a game changer that prepared me to be an entrepreneur. When I was nine, I started nagging him about a new bicycle. My cousin, Gary Martens, had just bought a brand-new bike, and I wanted one, too. I think it cost eight or nine dollars. Dad said, "Let me show you how to get your bike. I've got these four runt pigs. They're sickly, and one or two will probably die. But if you take really good care of them, two or three might live. It'll take you about six months but should earn you enough money for a bicycle.

"Oh, by the way," he added, "You're going to need some feed for those pigs, and you must pay for it. But I'll let you pay for it with labor. If you take care of this row of my pigs every day, I'll give you the feed for your four little runts."

Well, the happy ending to that story is that all four runts turned into big fat hogs. Price controls came off, and hogs were worth more than ever. When they sold, I ended up with enough money to buy 10 bicycles. But I bought one nice one, a Schwinn with headlight, horn, mud flaps and the works. So the next time I needed something, I didn't ask Dad for money. Instead, I asked him for an opportunity to take care of some pigs or do other chores. I was learning to provide labor in service to what his needs were to create wealth of my own! That lesson on wealth creation by using sweat equity was absolutely pivotal in my becoming a business thinker. **Life tip #10: Start with sweat equity.**

Experiences like this gave me the sense that I could create and be in control of my own economic destiny. I didn't need a handout. I could roll up my sleeves and do something. As a result, during my years growing up, I sold Christmas cards and candy, picked up pop bottles with Larry and city cousin Gary Martens, sold peanuts and ice cream at Tunis Speedway at the urging of a dear neighbor, Alice Kiewiet, an early mentor. Mary Lou Butz set me up as a jewelry salesperson while in high school. She was another of my early encouragers and cheerleaders with her mom, Gladys Schneiderman. I started a long history of being actively involved in raising enough money to buy the things I wanted. At 15 I saved more than the $365 needed to buy a 1949 Chevy that took me all the way through college.

The older I got, the more incrementally difficult activities Dad assigned me. I went from caring for the pigs and milking cows to driving tractors and trucks by the age of 11. As a result, I begin to climb up the ladder of understanding so that by the time I was 17, I was fairly well equipped to run the farm. In fact, Dad and Mom took off for a week and turned the whole farm over to me. Cows to milk. Eggs to gather. Pigs and cattle to feed and water. It gave me a great sense of confidence that there was nothing on this complex farm that I couldn't handle. It also fueled my desire to be a farmer.
Life tip #11: Create wealth by earning it.

Working alongside Dad also gave me a great interest in and knowledge about agriculture and the crops and livestock that he skillfully nurtured. While we were working, he might

be talking about things like priorities and what drove each season's workload. Hot summers and cold winters required very different preparations for cattle, hogs and poultry. How does a farm boy learn how to manage an integrated publishing company? Maybe it was by watching his dad manage three ages of dairy cattle, two of beef cattle and hogs at three stages of growth. That's 12 or more enterprises times four seasons totaling 48 different preparations as seasons change. That's 12 hours of work daily, 365 days a year. Planning, priorities, pacing and pricing were lessons from the barnyard that I would later apply in the boardrooms of Cedar Falls, Chicago, New York and London.
Life tip #12: Learn to manage complexity.

Dad also taught me to mix in a little fun with the sometimes dusty, dirty, stinky farm chores. He put a basketball hoop on the corn crib and one in the barn where he and his high school friend and teammate, Vade Force, taught me the basics of the game. Dad's pace: "Let's shoot a few baskets, boys." Then after 10 minutes: "Let's milk a few cows, boys. Merrill, throw down some hay from the middle window." Vade also taught me how to develop film and print pictures in his basement darkroom. That knowledge was helpful in journalism school.

My first vacation and first trip out of Iowa was with Aunt Theo (Dad's sister), Uncle Ray Martens and cousins Gary, Marlene and baby Francene. That's five people. Add Dad, Mom, Larry and me, and we had nine people in one car! But it was a big, pretty new 1947 Kaiser. Uncle Ray always drove good cars. Gas was 20 cents a gallon, so we must have saved lots of money traveling in one car.

Hanging Kettle Lake Resort in Minnesota gave us a glimpse into the past. Our icebox was provided with ice daily from the icehouse stacked full of layers of ice blocks separated by sawdust. There was a single light bulb hanging from the ceiling of the cabin. There were only two beds, so we kids slept under the kitchen table. There was no dining out, just picnic baskets of food. We learned to fish. This was my first taste of being away from home, on vacation, for a whole week. Hard summer work had its payday!

Life tip #13: Mix in a little fun.

Aunt Theo and Uncle Ray hosted Oster holiday gatherings with pot luck dinners and lots of great fellowship. They weren't the only extended family to impact me. Uncle Don and Aunt Donna Oster invested lots of time with Larry and me. A. B. Allen brought *Life, Look* and other magazines to our home. His son Jack visited me in college and let me talk him into becoming a landowner with me as his tenant. When Dad's Aunt Adda lost her son in World War II, Dad became her surrogate son. When Dad passed, I was the recipient of her visits, letters and encouraging phone calls.

Life wasn't always easy and fun. I watched Dad struggle to get money to move from renter to owner. I saw how he saved and planned and tried to figure out how he could buy land. Larry and I sat in the back of the car as he and Mom looked at different farms. As his dreams were fulfilled, we saw the great joy he got from having a farm in his own name. By the time Dad died in 1971, he owned 280 acres debt-free. I got my first "master's degree" in business watching him make that progress. He told me, "Farmers live poor but die rich," giving me insight into how farm families accumulate wealth — by owning land! They live from hand to mouth, then die with equity in a farm.

Bingo! He set off a time bomb in my life. That was better than a college course in economics, delivered in one short sentence!

Life tip #14: Buy land. Own your farm.

• • •

My home was the biggest influence in my early years, but as I grew older, there were people in other settings who had an impact on me. The main venues God used for these encounters in my life were the church, 4-H and high school.

My grandparents and parents were active participants in their respective local churches. They never segregated their Sunday activity from their weekday activity, so I grew up hearing about God and seeing Christianity lived out by people whose faith walk made them examples and pillars of strength in the community. They were consistently sought out for advice on matters of this life and the next. They had a quiet confidence about them that came from reading the Bible, prayer and guidance from a quiet voice they called the Holy Spirit.

I was only five years old when I caught the big vision that I was created by God and was so special in his eyes that he had a plan for me. But as my dear Grandma Carrie would pump up my ego with that powerful truth, she would pat the back of my head and add another simple truth: "But you're just a little sinner." Then she would follow that downer with the real clincher: "But Jesus died for you. Someday you must personally receive his gift of salvation, or it will never be yours."

Life tip #15: Get an eternal perspective.

I frequently attended Sunday School at the Walnut Street Baptist Church in Waterloo with Grandma Bessie. I remember sitting with my mouth open, spellbound by the beauty and drama of the stories I learned from the Bible week after week. I can still recall Dr. Ketcham on the platform creating a picture of the flood, telling how there were people swimming up to the ark after the rains started, but they were too late. "And if you don't accept Christ," he would warn, "you will be lost like they were."

I was encouraged to memorize Bible verses at Walnut Street Baptist, incentivized to memorize verses in the country school and challenged to win a Bible if I memorized verses in summer Bible school. The philosophical superstructure for my life was being shaped by truths from Scripture. I articulated this life philosophy much later in life as I made speeches to various groups around the country. But the building blocks were laid in the country school and at church. These are some of the key ideas and verses that stuck:

1. Jesus saves us to an eternal life. "For God so loved the world that he gave his one and only Son, that whoever believes in him shall not perish but have eternal life" (John 3:16).

   This verse is frequently referred to as "the gospel in a nutshell."

2. Love God, love others. Jesus replied: "'Love the Lord your God with all your heart and with all your soul and with all your mind.' This is the first and greatest commandment. And the second is like it: 'Love your neighbor as yourself'" (Matthew 22:37–39).

   Jesus himself called this the Great Commandment, folding the essence of the Ten Commandments into this one.

3. Make disciples. "Therefore go and make disciples of all nations, baptizing them in the name of the Father and of the Son and of the Holy Spirit" (Matthew 28:19).

   While we were learning this verse in Sunday

school, we were also singing a chorus that put the idea into music: "We are saved, saved to tell others of the Man of Galilee."

4. Love your wife. "Husbands, love your wives, just as Christ loved the church and gave himself up for her" (Ephesians 5:25).

5. Train your children. "Start children off on the way they should go, and even when they are old they will not turn from it" (Proverbs 22:6).

6. Do all as for the Lord. "And whatever you do, whether in word or deed, do it all in the name of the Lord Jesus, giving thanks to God the Father through him" (Colossians 3:17).

7. You can change the world. "I can do all this through him who gives me strength" (Philippians 4:13).

In total I probably recited 300 verses and received the approval of my Sunday school teacher, my daily vacation Bible school teacher, my fifth grade teacher, my mom, my grandmothers and the Lord.

Life tip #16: Memorize Bible verses; you'll need them.

I was eight years old when Dad got saved. It changed everything. He began taking the family to the Gospel Hall in Stout that my Grandpa and Grandma Smith had helped start years earlier. When I wasn't going with him, somebody would swing by and pick up Grandma, Larry and me. Sometimes we'd go four or five nights a week if there was a special series of gospel meetings. The preaching was the hellfire and brimstone stuff from circuit-riding preachers like Oliver Smith and Paul Elliott. Those two could rain down hellfire the likes of which I've never heard since. The fear they created in a kid's mind would probably be considered child abuse today. I remember waking up in the middle of the night thinking I was falling into a lake of fire. The Sunday School teacher at Stout was a fellow dairy farmer, Oscar Meyer. His first question when he walked into the classroom was, "Did anybody get saved this week?" I was well aware of the consequences of dying without a relationship with Christ!

My own conversion came years later at 13. I was sitting on a five-gallon pail under the steps in the basement while a storm raged outside. Shingles were flying across the yard. My dad was upstairs watching them, but he had sent Larry and me, my mother and my grandmother to the safety of the basement. That's where Grandma said to me, "Merrill, you've been thinking about this for a long time. You're trying to make something more out of it than really exists. Just believe in the Lord Jesus Christ, and you'll be saved."

At that moment, the weight of hundreds of Sunday School messages and sermons and family conversations about God fell on me all at once. I had accumulated lots of knowledge about God but had not personally accepted his gift of salvation. At that moment I took a step of faith and make him mine. In a split second I really believed that I moved from darkness into light. I said to Grandma, "Well, I believe! That means I'm saved!" She said, "Yes, it does. Run upstairs and tell your dad what just happened."

Life tip #17: Move beyond knowledge to belief.

So, I did. Dad was happy and we stayed up that night and talked for quite a while. The next morning before school, Grandma said to me, "Now you be sure to tell Jim Sluiter what happened to you." From the outset I was encouraged as an eighth grader to tell my story to another eighth grader. Jim and I grew up in the same church. When I told him I was now saved, he said, "What? You?"

Fast forward to when we were in college at Iowa State. Jim gives me a call and says, "Hey, Merrill. I got a friend here who's asking questions about the faith. You need to come over and lead him to the Lord." I said, "You went to the same Sunday School I did, Jim. You lead him to the Lord." To which he replied, "Merrill, get over here now! I'm not saved!" Although Jim's friend was unmoved by my words, Jim later became a Christian who had a strong influence on many others.

Life tip #18: Tell others what God has done for you.

• • •

My grandparents and parents provided the solid spiritual foundation upon which my life has been built. These six people have preceded me into their eternal heavenly life, but their memories and their visits to my thoughts and dreams are ongoing. Their passion for the Lord and their Christian-based family values had a profound impact on me. Their words and actions seemed small at the time but they set me on a course that led me from an Iowa farm to the inner circle of financial decision-makers around the globe and on to establishing Pinnacle Forum, a ministry that encourages and equips influential leaders to impact culture in world-changing ways.

I'm honored and humbled to say that the grace of God was poured into my life by these six pillars who created a culture of love, encouragement, achievement, service to others and a high view of the Bible and its Author.

Two

Early Education
Igniting Controversy and Change

Oster, this is the worst display of leadership I've ever seen.
— Mr. Runyon

A t the turn of the century in 1900, about 97 percent of Americans were directly or indirectly employed on farms. By the turn of the next century in 2000, only about 2 percent were so employed due to mechanization. I saw the wave of progress hit our community like a tidal wave in 1950. It was the final year of the threshing ring where neighboring farmers worked together and moved from one farm to the next to harvest the oat kernels from the fragile stalks. As Larry and I were playing in the front yard, we saw an approaching stream of tractors pulling bundle wagons, grain wagons, trucks and the big threshing machine that was the center of the action once harvest began.

Ten farmers showed up, most with their hired man or an older child or two. Some headed to the field to toss the oat shocks into the bundle wagons. Others anchored the big tractor whose power would throw the thresher into action.

One would haul the oats to a nearby bin. Two would stack the straw as fast as it flew out of the thresher. In the house, my mother and neighboring wives were preparing the noon feast for twenty men. Larry and I watched and listened to the final chords of an agricultural symphony.

The large threshing unit sucked in the bundles tossed in from both sides of the conveyor by sweating workers. The machine spit out harvested oats on one side and belched out a continuous blast of straw on the other. You could barely hear the putt-putt-putt sound of the two-cylinder John Deere tractors as they pulled bundle wagons from the field to the thresher. You had to walk out into the field to see the ultimate link to our past. There, one old neighbor brought his team of horses to pull his bundle wagon. He said, "Hup," and the horses advanced until he said, "Whoa!" We never saw horses doing fieldwork on the farm after that 1950 summer.

About 75 years earlier, Cyrus McCormick invented the mechanical mower and bundling machine called the binder that cut the oats and bundled it mechanically, allowing farmers to cut 20 acres a day with their reaper where one man could do a single acre by hand. Not much had changed in the way oats were harvested from the time of his invention until 1950. Larry and I were about to witness how one farmer, our Grandpa, influenced the decision-making process of a neighborhood to usher in an abrupt change in farming practices.

As the farmers took a noon break and ate their last piece of pie in picnic style dining under the shade of the trees in our front yard, Grandpa Jim Oster pulled in driving his Army surplus Jeep from World War II. He dropped out of the threshing ring because this was his first year as a combine owner. His new combine cut a six-foot swath of oats, threshed it, spit grain into a built-in tank and spread straw out the back. "I can do single-handedly what it takes you twenty guys all day to do," he chirped to my dad's embarrassment. "It's the wave of the future."

Life tip #19: Embrace change or get buried.

His picture of the future was dead right. The next year every farmer in the threshing ring either bought his own combine or contracted with someone who had one. Larry and I had a ringside seat to a wave of agricultural history that changed the way grain was harvested and laid the tracks for really large-scale farming. Instead of a six-foot swath, think 60 feet just 20 years later. Instead of 20 acres a day, think 300! Instead of a family farming 240 acres, think 2,400 just 30 years later. And today, yes, 24,000 acres under the control of each of my neighbors, Duane DeGrote and Dennis Krueger, near my hometown.

We saw the dam break in 1950. I was 10 years old. The small 160-acre farm was about to become history. Everything about farming was about to change. That dizzying pace of change would set up the opportunity for a new kind of information service. I was being positioned to fill that need.

At age 11, I joined the Eager Beavers 4-H club. 4-H clubs helped young people learn the basics of agriculture and live-stock management. It was here that I got my first leadership experience and my first mentoring outside the home. The club leaders were neighbors who cared enough to pick us up, take us to the meetings and spend time teaching us.

My first project was a heifer calf. I picked a nice black and white Holstein from a neighbor's stock and took care of it for about a year. But at the Butler County Fair, the judge placed my well-groomed calf dead last. Well, I came home from that disaster with a firm decision to get out of the dairy business. Based on my previous success with runt pigs, I decided to try hogs. Dad suggested I buy a couple female pigs from another neighbor and raise two litters. This time

I went over the hill in Dad's pickup, armed with some 4-H experience. They were teaching us to read the bulletins put out by Iowa State College. I had one that showed what a good pig should look like.

Louis Jurgenson turned me loose in his pigpen. I took a pail of grease and began to mark the pigs I thought looked the best. I narrowed it to the two best and brought them home in the back of Dad's pickup. They became the mother sows of my winning pigs — three championships in a row at the Butler County Fair. My brother took over my breeding stock and won championships the next couple of years. Those pigs not only won ribbons, but they also generated cash for us. We learned how to do enterprise analysis and to keep track of every dollar we spent.

In later 4-H years, I branched out and did projects with poultry, rabbits and beef. I drove an old 1944 Chevy pickup loaded with every kind of animal to the county fair with brother Larry and close friend Ron Kiewiet. We returned home with lots of ribbons, lots of experience and a new level of confidence.

Life tip #20: If at first you don't succeed, try again.

It was at the Butler County Fair where I made my first and last attempt at being a tough guy. As I was walking past a carnival booth, one of the "carnies" as we called the workers, made a smart comment about my not having the guts to throw darts at his balloons.

"Oh, yeah. You wanna make something of it?" I challenged. "Meet me behind the hog barn." I walked to the back of the hog barn, out of sight of anybody who could see me clean this guy's clock. As he approached I stuck out my chest. He stuck out his switchblade knife!

I stepped back, glanced for an opening to make a dash if necessary and said, "You win! Game over! New Jersey, one.

New Hartford, zero." His sneer turned to an arrogant grin, and thank God, he decided not to stab me.

Never did that again.

Life tip #21: Pick your fights carefully.

I thought having success in speechmaking at the county fair meant I would have no trouble at the state fair in Des Moines. I expected to get a blue ribbon for a verbal demonstration on contour farming. However, I did not prepare. I stumbled through my presentation. I came off the platform at the state fair thinking, oh boy, I really blew it. I did. It was a red, not a blue ribbon—second place. That experience caused me to always overprepare for a speech. In the several hundred speeches I was to give professionally later on in life, I never had that same sinking feeling coming off a platform. It was a lesson well learned—one that was to earn some handsome speaking fees in the decades ahead.

Life tip #22: Be prepared before you step on the platform.

It was 4-H that brought two very important men into my life: the county extension director, Ivan Wickner, and his assistant, Norville Mosher. These guys took a personal interest in me while I was learning how to develop speeches, turn those speeches into demonstrations and judging contest presentations where 4-H'ers learned how to rank a class of cattle or hogs and to give the reasons for their decisions in front of a panel of judges. We judged the livestock. They judged us.

Ivan and Norville took me to various county hog shows and fairs across the middle of America when my dad was busy farming. They taught me how to be a good judge of livestock. They coached me on how to make good decisions and express those decisions in a very crisp manner so as to persuade a judge. These guys showed up again later in my life. Ivan became an executive at Pioneer Seed Company and a presenter at Pro Farmer seminars. Norville became a farmer and longtime member of our Professional Farmers of America.

Here I was, still in high school, bringing back ideas from the county extension service on how to be a better farmer, learning how to practice those ideas and demonstrate them to others, including my dad. That was part of the wisdom behind the land grant college system and the 4-H program that came out of it—a way to transfer knowledge from the university to local farmers through the 4-H'ers.

For example, one time I was learning how to save baby pigs, I gave a demonstration at home to some 4-H'ers on how to make little guard rails across the corner of a square pig pen to keep the mama sow from laying on her pigs. My dad overheard me. The next fall I noticed he'd put those guard rails in his pens. The same thing happened after I demonstrated the value of terraces. One day I got off the school bus and ran out to see what my dad was doing in the field. He had hired a guy with a road grader and they were making a terrace on the only hill on the farm following a demonstration I had done on the topic. My dad was not only a good teacher, but he was very teachable.

Life tip #23: Be a lifelong learner.

My involvement with 4-H included serving as a county and state officer. In my freshman year of college, I was selected as one of the two outstanding 4-H boys in the state of Iowa. George White was the other. We were chosen to attend the national 4-H conference in Washington, D.C., and hear President Dwight Eisenhower open the conference. That was one of the highlights of my teen years. George and I became fraternity brothers and lifelong friends.

The other big teen experience that shaped my career

was winning the Farmers' Grain Dealer Association public speaking contest. Larry Anton, a fellow 4-H'er, told me I could increase my chances of getting a college scholarship if I got involved in speech contests. I entered the Iowa Farm Grain Dealer speaking contest along with 75 contestants from all over the state. I won, which was a defining moment that gave me an audience and name recognition. I gave my speech to an audience of 2,000 people in Iowa's Veteran's Auditorium in Des Moines as a result of winning the contest—the first large audience I'd ever spoken to. It was a scary thrill, but also a stepping stone from one level to the next. It gave me the confidence to continue with public speaking and garnered invitations to local farmer co-op annual meetings for the next two years while in high school and college.

Over the course of my career, I've honed my speaking skills. I've spoken to thousands of people in dozens of countries. From countless platforms I've taught farmers about buying farmland, commodity traders about the futures market and leaders about using their God-given influence to be change agents in the world. The latter has been in connection with a group I helped found called Pinnacle Forum. More on all of that later. It all started with 4-H.

• • •

I attended New Hartford High School, graduating in 1958. I excelled in every sport the school offered—two: basketball and baseball. My moment of sports glory was playing two minutes in the 1956 state tournament as a 15-year-old bench warming sophomore. I fouled once, shot twice and missed both. The team lost and we placed third.

New Hartford High School was small enough—about 90 kids—that I was able to participate in everything from chorus and singing solos to public speaking and writing for the school paper. As a junior, I was editor of the editorial page of the *Hawkeye*, our school newspaper. That job got me in hot water.

I got into my first editorial controversy by voicing my opinion in writing. I wrote an editorial, probably too sharply worded, castigating the superintendent and principal for letting kids from other schools pass us up in college because they had trigonometry and advanced algebra and we didn't. The newspaper advisor, Mr. Cuthbertson, took the editorial to the principal's office before the article ever got out. I was censored! "This is not going in the paper," the principal, Mr. Runyon, told me, as he dressed me down but good. "What are you doing, Merrill? You can't write this way in the high school newspaper. You're embarrassing the administration of the school." Heaven forbid that a high school kid would embarrass an elder for his incredible lack of foresight!

I went home steaming and told Dad that my editorial had been thrown into the wastebasket by the principal. I had no way of getting my message out. "Don't complain to me about it," Dad said. "Tell someone who can make a difference. Go over the hill to our neighbor Herman Hemingway. He's the president of the school board."

I did just that and shared my concerns with Herman. I told him how ridiculous I thought it was that I should be censored and that the school didn't teach advanced algebra and trigonometry. He listened to my rant, and when I finished, he said, "Calm down, Merrill. It's hard for students to make changes, but don't worry about it." I didn't hear anything more about it, but the following fall the school offered trigonometry and advanced algebra. God used me as a stimulus for change, giving me the confidence that I could make a difference in larger settings.

Life tip #24: You can change your world—speak up!

I was an above-average student but not outstanding because I always had a lot of other things to do. From the time I was 16, in addition to my farm chores, I had a 20- to 25-hour-a-week job at the Benson Creamery. And I was involved in 4-H, sports and many other activities such as class plays. I didn't have time to do much homework. I could get a B without trying and an A with a little extra effort. I ended up third in my graduating class of 13.

I was not afraid to challenge conventional thinking or advice I was given in high school. My basketball coach, Mr. Spurbeck, drove by Benson Creamery and noticed my car out front at 7:30 a.m. "Oster, if you want to play on this basketball team, I don't want to see your car at that creamery." I didn't believe in either-or choices, so I parked my car behind the creamery and kept working. Spurbeck never saw my car in front of the creamery again. I started every game as his forward. I was five feet ten. Our guards were five feet eight. Our big center, friend Alvin Kyhl, was a towering six feet one.

I had a pretty good performance in the deportment category until the last week of school my senior year. The town honored the senior class at a breakfast, and afterward I invited three of my best friends to jump in the car and skip school. Dale Gast, Alvin Kyhl, Ken Harken and I just drove around Cedar Falls and Waterloo. It was boring. School would have been more fun.

The next day we were called into the principal's office. This wasn't the first time, but it was the first time I remember hearing the word leadership associated with my name. Mr. Runyon said, "Oster, this is the worst display of leadership I've ever seen." What he said put the idea in my mind that I might be a leader. God uses the strangest things sometimes to plant little seeds that blossom into confidence.

Watching and learning from my dad made me want to be

a farmer after high school. When I told my mom this, she said, "Oh no, you're not." Mom was a schoolteacher who valued education. "You might farm someday, but you're going to college first." My dad was sitting there at the table, and he agreed. "Try something else and then come back to the farm if that's still what you want. Keep your options open."

No question I would go to college; it was just a matter of which one. I had regularly attended Iowa State College functions as part of 4-H field days. I also met people from Iowa State who were livestock judges at county fairs. In my senior year, several of us 4-H'ers went to Ames for a career day. Dr. Louis Thompson gave us a briefing on various career options. He went down the list of 20 different majors within the College of Agriculture. When he said agricultural journalism, my heart leapt because he explained that journalism combined writing, public speaking and public relations. Right then I knew I wanted to study journalism. That must have been a nudge and a shot of insight from the Holy Spirit because before that moment my trajectory had been toward engineering.

When I got home, I told Dad I'd decided to be an agricultural journalist. He said, "You're gonna be a what?" I had to explain to him what an agricultural journalist was, even though I didn't have a very clear picture myself. But Dad and Mom were supportive.

When it came to other people in my life, I got more questions than support for the journalism decision. My high school math teacher was totally taken aback. My science teacher thought I was nuts. I was good in math, and they thought I should become an engineer. This was the fall of 1957. Russia had launched the Sputnik satellite. The country was going bananas over mathematics and engineering because we had to catch up to the Russians. However, by this point I had enough confidence that I could say to my teachers, "I know what I want to do in life." I was totally confident in the decision I had made on campus that day and I hit the ground running.

Life tip #25: Follow your inner guide—the Holy Spirit.

• • •

Nearing my 80s I can now look back on a diverse and fruitful career. I became an agricultural journalist, then independent publisher and business owner, and as a sideline, I started farming to satisfy that original passion. The lessons I learned in and around the barn taught by my dad and other influential men shaped my value system and work ethic, as it did a generation of other farm boys and girls. It's one of the reasons why so many heads of banks and major organizations in Chicago and New York during the '50s, '60s and '70s had their roots in agriculture.

I've given my "lessons from the barn" speech many times over the years. Those lessons are rooted in a physical place. Let me show you around and highlight just a few of the lessons that shaped my early life:

As you step over the doorsill, take a look down. It is a four-by-four worn almost round by family footsteps—Dad's, Granddad's and all the kids'. These weren't random footsteps. Every six o'clock for 40 years, men and women stepped across that sill to feed and milk the cows.

Regularity that breeds discipline is one of the characteristics that opens the door to success. No one ever told us we were learning discipline. We never thought there was another way. We knew the cows had to be milked at the same time every day for maximum production, and we needed every ounce of cream we could get if we were to afford new shoes and a new plaid shirt to start school.

Life tip #26: Develop discipline.

Step over the sill and come down the six steps, and you're in the separator room. The separator room was a happy spot. When the day's activities focused on this room, it meant the milking was done, and it was about time to head for the supper table. While changing pails one day, I spilled part of a pail of milk, only to get a stern admission that spilling is wasteful: "Skim milk has value. Don't waste it. Now don't cry over spilled milk. Just don't spill it again."
Life tip #27: Become frugal.

Slide the door to your right and step into the cow barn. Twenty-six stanchions. Twenty-six cows to milk when every station was full. Walk down the aisle to the right. Next to the wall there were calf pens. Pens that needed regular cleaning. Pause at the gate to the last pen.

I was 14, getting ready to start cleaning a pen that didn't look like it needed cleaning. Testing my newfound manhood, I asked Dad condescendingly, "Why do you want to waste our time cleaning this pen today?" Without any anger Dad said, "This pen needs cleaning. Two of us can do it in fifteen minutes, or I can do it alone in thirty." He instinctively knew when it was time to quit telling a boy what to do and begin making him responsible for his own decisions. I had a choice, and he was giving me the freedom to make it even at the cost of his personal sacrifice. The pen was clean in 15 minutes.
Life tip #28: Make informed decisions.

Just outside the barn door is the cow yard. The cows would wade through knee-deep mud every spring. Then one summer Dad announced we were going to borrow a cement mixer and each day pour a six-foot strip of concrete across the cow yard until we had it covered. Now that's hard work. After the first day, we were just about dead. The next morning, Dad said to me and my brother, Larry, "Boys, when we get this strip done today, we'll go to Waterloo to the Byrnes Park swimming pool."

Now with a goal in mind, the sand shovel only weighed half as much. The work seemed bearable, and we finished that day's strip of concrete an hour earlier, knowing that the heat of the day would soon give way to the cool water of the pool. Dad's overall goal was to get the cows out of the mud, but he gave Larry and me a goal we could realize immediately.

Life tip #29: Set goals and reward service.

I keep a memory bank of Dad's sayings. These weren't things he preached at us but insights he shared with us as we worked side by side:

"The game isn't over until the final out." That was Dad's way of saying don't quit even when you're way behind.

"A little extra effort makes the difference between mediocrity and excellence." That was Dad's way of saying good wasn't good enough. Excellence is our goal.

"If a job is worth doing, it's worth doing well." That was Dad's way of holding up the high value of quality work.

"While you're doing one job, think ahead to the next one." That was Dad's way of helping a son set priorities.

"Do unto others as you would have them do unto you." That was Dad teaching theology even before I knew the words were from the Bible.

Life tip #30: Let the words of your elders settle in your soul.

• • •

I'm thankful for the role models and mentors who were a regular part of my early life: grandparents, parents, 4-H leaders, teachers. And for those who had an apparently glancing impact but whom the Lord used to nudge me in the right direction at a hundred different forks in the road. Sometimes one powerful sentence out of the mouth of an unsuspecting influencer pointed the way to the next phase of my future.

At this point, the path God had for me led to Iowa State College (now Iowa State University), to FarmHouse Fraternity, George White, Jerry Carlson, Craig Simcox, Dallas McGinnis and Harry Heath, to name a few.

Three

Solid Foundation
Putting Faith into Action

Oster, you claim to be fishing for a Christian wife;
I suggest you cast your net in a pond known for Christians.
— Craig Simcox

I packed my 1949 Chevy with most everything I owned and drove off to Iowa State College in the fall of '58. Because of my public speaking success and being named one of the top 4-H'ers in Iowa, FarmHouse Fraternity recruited me directly out of high school, a FarmHouse first.

They had their reasons. God had his.

The Lord put me in the FarmHouse for multiple reasons, especially for the people I would meet there. George White was one. I was outspoken about my faith, and one evening, a few guys came to listen to me and another guy chat about eternal matters in a "bull session." Next thing I knew, we had five guys, and it was midnight. By two o'clock, just George and I were left. He said, "You know, I think you and I believe in exactly the same way."

We became close friends. For the next several months, we challenged each other to get up every morning to pray and read Scripture before going to class. George and I began to learn how to really pray and to take Bible reading seriously. He went on to pastor a church and influence thousands.

But the giant influencer on campus was my pledge father, Jerry Carlson. He was a few years older than me and became like an older brother. One day we were at the mailbox and he said, "Look here, Merrill," and showed me a check for $15 from the *Poultry Tribune.* "You mean journalism can pay even while you're in college?" I asked. "That's what it does," he replied.

We talked about ways I could sell stories, so even before I took my first writing class, at Jerry's urging, I had already sold several magazine articles to the *Wallace's Farmer.* Before I took my first class on radio broadcasting, I was broadcasting live daily on WOI, thanks to Jerry's connections. I paid my way through college with these and various other part time jobs. I did everything from sweeping carpets and washing pots and pans at FarmHouse to selling ads for KASI radio and running a highly profitable dance photography business. I took pictures of couples attending a college-wide or fraternity dance. It was almost obligatory if you took your date to a dance to have your picture taken with her. One night I left Memorial Union after a homecoming dance with $3,300 in my pocket. Now that was a serious amount of money in the day when a full year's tuition at Iowa State was $1,500.

Jerry invited me to a church in Ames where he was preaching on Sunday morning as a part time fill-in. There I saw firsthand a man integrating academic interests with spiritual pursuits. Jerry was mentoring me just by letting me see him in action.

Life tip #31: Find a good mentor and listen.

Jerry introduced me to another FarmHouse man, Jerry Brady, who led me to the WOI Radio job. I applied and was hired, though still a freshman. My boss, Dallas McGinnis, was a familiar voice I had heard growing up on a steady diet of KWWL radio before his move to WOI radio in Ames. Dallas taught me how to gather information, put it together and deliver a message. "Find the human interest in the story," he would say. "Connect with the audience's needs." I spent the next two years working with Dallas, honing my writing and broadcasting skills.

Radio work started at 5:30 a.m. The station claimed the broadcast went to 200,000 listeners, but I think 180,000 of them were Holstein cows. Most farmers who milked turned on WOI for some music and chitchat to calm the animals. Our broadcasts informed the farmers on the weather forecast, news from the grain markets and from around the world. I reported on the Cuban Missile Crisis, the Gary Powers capture by the Russians and all the headline stories of the era.

One morning on the way home from my broadcast, Jan Hutchenson, a friend from the neighboring sorority shouted, "Merrill, your house is on fire." I rushed to the smoke-filled FarmHouse, but the firemen wouldn't let me in. I was the only guy in the house who lost everything. Every book, every stitch of clothes. I drove home to rural Cedar Falls where Dad and Mom took me to Waterloo to buy new clothes at Delorbes, Wards and Penny's, then to Boysens in Cedar Falls for shoes. I returned to school and grabbed a snack at the student union. While I was eating, someone stole my brand-new hat! That was the last straw! At that point I reached an emotional low. I got the picture that God was speaking. But why? "What's up, Lord?" I began to pray with greater intensity.

Life tip #32: God speaks, sometimes in a crisis.

Later as I'm walking back to the FarmHouse to assess the fire damage, an acquaintance I knew from the Waterloo

Gospel Hall, Craig Simcox, saw me and asked, "What's going on?" When I told him my fraternity house had a fire, he said, "I believe there's an open bed in the rooming house where I'm staying." Hours later I moved in. That's what God had up his sleeve!

That first night in the rooming house, Craig said, "Merrill, some of us get together at the end of the day to pray and read Scripture for about an hour. Do you want to join us?" I went from praying with George to joining Craig and a few others, extending my biblical support group. He also invited me to his church on Sundays, which I attended for many months. We frequently had lunch in his parents home where Claire Simcox, Craig's dad, encouraged and answered theological questions, and in his own way mentored me.

One of those confidence-building, one-line statements that impacted me in 1961 came from the regionally famous preacher, Oliver Smith. I had delivered a five-minute talk at a Bible conference. As I stepped off the stage, I heard Oliver say to the man sitting next to him, "That young man has a gift." I began to think about my responsibility to develop and use my gift of evangelism, the ability to tell others about Jesus.

My life-changing experiences at churches, the Farm-House and rooming house with Bible study, prayer and peer interaction on spiritual issues formed the basis for what I would later replicate with Pinnacle Forum. And my interaction with guys like Jerry Carlson and Dallas McGinnis would shape my business career. Harry Heath, my advisor, labored to help me develop my broadcast skills. He also tried to get me to slow down and focus on one or two activities. He was unsuccessful on that score.

Before he graduated, Jerry invited me to ride along on an interview trip for a story he was doing. We talked about the future of communications in agriculture and how great it would be to deliver important decision-making news to the American farmer in real time. The technology to do that didn't exist back then; it was just a dream. But that conversation planted seeds in the back of our heads in 1960 that took root 13 years later when I recruited him from *Farm Journal* to join me in creating a new kind of agricultural information service, Professional Farmers of America.

Life tip #33: Dream big, but get a job.

The FarmHouse fire triggered several high-impact events. I'd been praying since I was probably 15 years old for a Christian wife and dating actively. Had dating been a varsity sport, I would have lettered all three years in college. None of the girls I was dating seemed to fit my description of a born-again believer. Craig heard me praying for a godly woman one night and said, "Oster, you claim to be fishing for a Christian wife; I suggest you cast your net in a pond known for Christians." That was the best advice I ever got in college.

While trolling around a Bible conference in Hitesville, Iowa, a few weeks later, I cast a glance toward Carol Dempster, the cutest blonde in the room. The Osters and Dempsters knew each other from the Stout Gospel Hall. Carol was the middle sister in a family of three, but now she was all grown up. I asked to drive her home. (It was only 20 miles out of the way!) Another important seed had been planted.

Life tip #34: Let your action follow your prayer.

• • •

I graduated from Iowa State in under three years and was headed to the University of Wisconsin in Madison for my master's in agricultural journalism. That summer I recalled overhearing Dad say to Mom, "That Carol Dempster sure is a nice girl," loud enough for me to hear. It was the first time he'd ever commented on someone I dated. The Lord used Dad's words to alert me to the fact Carol just might be the person I had been praying for.

I saw Carol at my brother's graduation reception, and we went out that very night and talked about our future plans. After a few more dates, the Holy Spirit impressed me that Carol was the woman I was going to marry. I believed the Lord wanted us together, but I had to convince her I wasn't just a college boy home for the summer looking for a good time. I must have succeeded because after a series of dates to parks, lakes and caves in Northern Iowa, mostly free stuff, I proposed, and she accepted.

Life tip #35: When you find her, never let her go.

We were married on June 1, 1962. I finished my master's degree that month at the University of Wisconsin, and Carol completed her degree in X-ray technology a year later. I moved her into a garden apartment rented for $70 a month that she had not seen. To this day she refers to it as a basement apartment because when I carried her over the threshold, she looked up and saw dripping water pipes. Anyway, it was what we could afford.

We started praying about my next job when she completed her degree. I'd been working at the American Society of Agronomy editing *Crops and Soils* magazine while waiting for Carol to graduate. I was pretty bored being surrounded by agronomists who couldn't teach me anything journalistically, so I spent lots of time with the circulation manager, Chuck Lewandowski. We talked about promoting the magazine, and I began to learn the direct mail marketing side of the publishing industry.

There are a few concepts in business that produce outsized results. One of them was revealed to me while sitting in our 1955 Chevy waiting for Carol to complete her afternoon class. I was doing a subscription spreadsheet by hand, and a light bulb turned on in my mind as I saw the difference between recurring revenue generators and one-time revenue generators. I saw that a subscriber who renews his $50 subscription every year for 10 years is worth $500 with very little cost to renew per year. However, a customer who pays $50 to attend a seminar that must be recreated from scratch every year generates much less profit, maybe $5 per seminar or $50 for 10 annual events.

I discussed my insight with Chuck, who helped me see how to use direct mail to build an ongoing revenue stream of subscribers. There is a very sophisticated science to direct mail that isn't taught in college. I had to learn it on the job from experts like Chuck and others. That knowledge would become one of the secrets that gave our companies a competitive edge in future business startups.

Life tip #36: Know the lifetime value of a customer.

I sent out inquiry letters while in Madison and got job offers from Chicago, Washington, D.C., New York, and yes, Woodstock, Illinois. That one had a God gift written all over it. Carol and I got excited about it because Woodstock was only 25 miles from Lake Geneva, Wisconsin. For the past months we'd been traveling from Madison to Lake Geneva to attend Lake Geneva Bible Chapel. Carol's dad had introduced us to two men who ministered there, Ray Routely and Dan Dunnett. We were being mentored by men who were gifted pastors. Now we could be even closer.

Ray and Laura Routely got us involved in the church. They had us over to their house and showed us what the gift of hospitality looked like. They had a wonderful family and were a great example to Carol and me in the early years of our marriage and for 40 years thereafter. Just before we would leave their house, Ray usually stuck a book in my hand and said, "Merrill, read this." Two weeks later he would ask, "What'd you think of that book?" He didn't just pass out Christian books; he expected me to read and then interact with him.

Life tip #37: Study to grow spiritually.

The job offer in Woodstock, Illinois, came from John Strohm Associates. John was an entrepreneur, independent publishing consultant and one of the outstanding agricultural writers of the era. He had been nominated for a Pulitzer Prize. He was an international journalist with many articles appearing in *Reader's Digest*. He had just started *National Wildlife* magazine. He had a reputation for being a workaholic and a real taskmaster. This didn't scare me off but made me think, If he's a tough son of a gun to work for, I'll bet he can teach me something.

Life tip #38: Learn from the best.

John produced a million-circulation quarterly magazine, *Ford Farming*, and another half million-circulation annual publication, *Ford Almanac*, with his only other assistant in Woodstock, Cliff Ganschow. I was hired as an associate editor, and we moved to Woodstock in June 1963. Carol and I saw this as a real miracle. An answer to prayer and evidence that God was leading in our lives.

My major responsibility was writing for *Ford Farming* magazine. I started doing regional stories, then lead stories and wound up doing all the stories in *Ford Farming* as its managing editor. I bought manuscripts for stories I didn't have time to run down myself. We subscribed to every farm magazine in America and several from Europe. I handled the clipping file of good ideas and information resources from around the world. What a fantastic opportunity. I read and read and read and took stuff home at night and read some more. This night work probably didn't help our marriage any, but Carol was very tolerant. I was accumulating knowledge and contacts that would serve me in good stead later.

With two degrees in journalism, I still had a lot to learn about writing. John would take my work, edit it and hand it back. He revised copy with a red pencil and gave my prose a bloodbath. "The same thing in half the words," he would say. "Just get to the nub of an issue in the fewest possible words." That statement has stuck with me as I've edited my associates' writing, and even my own over the years since then.

Life tip #39: Just get to the nub of the story.

I was also learning how to put ideas on paper for our other clients like Terra Chemicals and International Minerals and Chemicals Co. I learned how to make presentations in a way that impressed people in the advertising business. I found myself at age 23 regularly sitting in front of the PR director of the tractor division of Ford Motor Company in Dearborn, Michigan, telling him what should be in the next issue of *Ford Farming*.

John taught me that if you want to know what the future holds, you have to spend time with the top 1 percent in a particular field. In five or 10 years, the whole world would be moving in the direction and adopting ideas they are using now. Consequently, I became very selective in whom I interviewed. Not only the top farmers but also the best economists, the best agronomists, the best folks in the various subsets of business and agriculture.

My job included traveling all over America interviewing outstanding farmers for the Ford Almanac Farm Efficiency Awards Program. Fresh out of college, I was getting a deeper education from some of the best agribusiness leaders in America. I began to get a clear picture of a group of innovators

in agriculture who were much more sophisticated than the average farmer. I recognized early on that this elite group was not being well served by the agricultural media. I was beginning to see an economic opportunity unfolding.
Life tip #40: Know the top 1 percent.

John spent a lot of time personally encouraging and guiding me. He took Carol and me to dinner and made sure we got connected and involved in the Woodstock community. We watched Super Bowl I in the Strohm home. He put me on a committee that led to Woodstock becoming an all-American city. There I met Frances Kuhn, a Woodstock leader, and later became her campaign manager. She was elected the first woman mayor of a city of more than 5,000 in Illinois. I became a charter member of the Woodstock Rotary Club. And when the ambulance company left town, I co-chaired a campaign to raise $20,000 to buy our own rescue truck and train a volunteer squad. I was trained along with several others to be rescue squad personnel. These turned out to be trial runs for service and ministry projects yet to come! John got my community involvement ball rolling.

Carol and I had an open Bible in our home and read it daily around the breakfast table. We were introduced to a week-long Family Bible Camp at Lake Koronis in Minnesota. It was a long trip from Woodstock to Lake Koronis, so an overnight stop was often part of our travel plans. Such was the case on July 20, 1969. Paul and Donna McCullagh, Carol's sister and brother-in-law, and their two girls, Paula and Janet, were traveling with us. We piled into one hotel room to watch Neil Armstrong take his first step on the moon on TV. It was a stunning fulfillment of a promise President Kennedy had made—one that I reported on as a broadcaster on WOI in Ames a few years earlier.

The technology that came out of the space initiative in

the next several years changed the way we did everything. Computers, handheld calculators, fax machines, satellite dishes, cell phones were on the drawing board.

Carol and I deepened our involvement with Lake Geneva Bible Chapel. I became the song leader, Sunday school superintendent, treasurer, whatever they needed from me over the years. And in each of the activities I worked closely with Ray Routley, Dan Dunnett and Paul Sapp. These men suggested Carol and I take Bible correspondence courses, which we did from Emmaus Bible School. These courses took us through the basics from salvation to the great doctrines of the Bible and gave us a deeper understanding of the Word.

Ray taught me an important spiritual lesson: "Merrill, there's no higher level of lifework than serving God's people." And I got to thinking, God's people aren't all in the local church. Most of the farmers I'm serving are also God's people in the larger body of Christ, his universal church. So I began to focus my thoughts on serving others as opposed to being so career-focused. That paradigm shift caused me to think about the farmers I was interviewing. What do these guys need? What can I bring to them that will be of benefit? How can I take good ideas from one part of the country and drop them into someone else's thought process?

Life tip #41: Serve your church and community.

This line of thinking informed a 10-page memo I wrote to John Strohm about a farm organization that would serve the top 1 percent of American agriculture. This was the genesis of what later became Top Farmers of America. The memo contained the intellectual body for the newsletter called *Top Farmer Intelligence*. John launched Top Farmers of America. I thought I was a shoo-in to be the editor. Then I got one of the big disappointments of my early journalistic life. John hired a man who was 10 years older than I was and paid him twice as much as me to execute the newsletter idea, for which I was partially responsible. I realized I was only 27 years old, so I put up with the disappointment for the next year until the newsletter was finally turned over to me in 1968. But I decided the day I got passed over that I wasn't going to put all my eggs in this one career basket. I needed to branch out.

Life tip #42: Keep your options open.

My first attempt at my own business in Woodstock was as a Shaklee products distributer. It was a total bust. I closed it down after a year. We had unsold boxes stacked of Basic H in our basement for the next 10 years!

My second attempt was more successful. To supplement my salary, John allowed me to do freelancing. I started my own freelancing business and sold about $4,000 worth of articles per year to farm publications around the country. We also bought our first farm in Iowa in 1967. Carol and I traveled back there on weekends, further whetting our appetite to return to our Iowa roots someday, probably to farm and write.

The morning I signed the deal for the 80-acre farm in New Hartford, I was eating lunch at Mom's table when a young man from the neighboring town approached me. "I understand you bought the Hensey farm," he said. "I'd like to go farming. I'll work on a salary. I'll go fifty-fifty. I'll do whatever." That's how Steve Shoemaker became my general farm manager. This was one of those God things. A stranger hears on the street that a farm has been sold and he wants to work on it with me. I could have said, "No. I'm still thinking about it." But I said yes on the spot and never regretted it.

When I told Dad I'd bought the Hensey farm, he said, "You did what? Of all the places in the world you could have bought. You ever drive by that farm and see all the sand? You should have waited for the Belz farm. " He chewed me out for what he thought was a big mistake. But he went from chastising me to saying just a few days later, "Well, you're going to need some equipment. I just bought an old disk for twenty-five dollars at an auction. You can have it. If you're going to farm a sandy farm you will need some old equipment."

About six months later, the Belz farm came up for sale, and I bought that also. I kept buying land on a shoestring with 5 or 10 percent down and convincing the owners to carry the credit. I sold off the building site on the farm to lower my land cost. Things were falling into place.

Life tip #43: Take pie when pie is passed.

• • •

One of the more eventful things that took place while I worked for John Strohm was the chance to lead a delegation of American farmers on a three-week agricultural mission around the world in January 1969. It was one of the highlights of my early journalistic life. I led this delegation of highly influential agribusiness men, members of Top Farmers of America, to Japan, Hong Kong, India, Israel, Pakistan, Thailand and England. It was a time to contemplate how I wanted to spend the rest of my journalistic career.

The squalid conditions in Pakistan and Thailand were stunning, but they were trumped by the views and smells on the back streets of India. Limp, fly-covered babies hanging over their mothers' shoulders left images permanently engraved in our minds. But it was in a wheat field in northern India where we found hope. We met Norman Borlaug, an internationally known wheat breeder who grew up in Cresco, Iowa, a few miles from my hometown. He would go on to win a Nobel Prize. This father of the Green

Revolution told me, "Demonstrate a better way and these Indian farmers will adopt it in a few years. Farmers are pretty darned smart, whether in Iowa or India."

The 15 agribusiness couples on that trip became friends, advisors and mentors. On the long bus trips, plane and train rides I peppered them with questions on how they got started and what they did to finance their various enterprises. At the end of our time together, I overheard one farmer say to another, "I don't think that young man is going to be with Strohm much longer. He's got the talent to move on." This boosted my confidence. It was another one of those random comments that confirmed what the Lord was leading me to do.

Another confidence-booster came from a subsequent speaking engagement set up by Max Shaul, one of the New York leaders on the trip. Max invited me to speak at the New York Governor's Conference in February 1970. The preceding speaker, Governor Nelson Rockefeller, was rumored to be a presidential candidate at the time. As he spoke, hundreds of women sitting next to their husbands looked down, concentrating on their knitting. He received a polite applause before I was introduced.

I gave the audience my optimistic view of the world. One by one I noticed the knitters stopped and shifted their attention to this 30-year-old speaker. I got a standing ovation, in stark contrast to Rockefeller's tepid reception.

Max was beaming. As a leading farmer in the state, his reputation was on the line for recommending me as a speaker. "Merrill, you nailed it," he exclaimed. I had upstaged the governor! Max was vindicated. I was three years from launching Professional Farmers of America. Max gave me encouragement to pursue my dream and became a charter member of Professional Farmers of America a few years later. It was one of those incidents in my life where seemingly small stuff, Max and the New York audience, were used by God to give me a shot of confidence, pushing me to the next stage in my life.

Life tip #44: Take a career assessment break.

Many years later, while receiving the Entrepreneur of the Year award in Iowa, Governor Branstad commented to me as I sat down from my acceptance speech. "I am sure glad I didn't have to face you in my reelection campaign!" He went on to become the Ambassador to China. I went on to serve American farmers and futures traders worldwide. I would not trade my role for his. We were each called by God to serve in uniquely different ways. And, as another of my mentors on that 1969 trip advised me, "I would rather have the ear of the governor than be one!" Another of those one-liners that provided a unique perspective as I sorted through options for the future.

By now Carol and I had two children. David was born in 1964 and Leah in 1966. My parents and Carol's parents frequently traveled to Woodstock to visit. They were very supportive and very happy to engage with the grandkids. But Carol and I wanted our parents to have a similar influence on our children that our grandparents had had on us, so we began to pray about moving back to Iowa.

Ever since my experiences with George White and Craig Simcox at Iowa State, I'd taken to praying on my knees. It became a thread that would wind through my life. The night Carol and I got married, I asked, "Would you mind starting a tradition?" From then on we ended our days in prayer on our knees. We did the same with our children when they came along. I can recall David yelling down the hall, "Come on, Dad. It's time to pray."

Twenty years later I was in David's house one night and I heard my grandson Philip yell down the stairs, "Come on, Dad. It's time to pray." It brought tears to my eyes as I realized that this tradition was being handed down to the next generation. Prayer always bathed our decisions and striking out on our own would be a big one.

I could also pray just fine on my feet. One weekend when Carol and I were visiting my folks in Iowa, I took an early morning prayer walk up the hill on the gravel road that divided their farm. I prayed out loud, something I don't normally do. "Lord, I'm contemplating a move at this stage in my career. I'd like to go on my own. I probably don't have the wherewithal to do it but I'd like to. Please help me decide if we should take this risk."

As I reached the top of the hill and started down, I felt this overwhelming closeness with the Lord. I didn't hear an audible voice, but a warm, confident feeling came over me, and I felt I was being told years before Nike coined the slogan "Just do it." I came down the hill and told Carol. "Well," she said, "wherever you go, I'll follow. I feel good about returning to Iowa, too." Her validation was vital.
Life tip #45: Validate your answers to prayer, then act.

I returned to the office in Woodstock and announced to my immediate superior, Cliff Ganschow, that I would be leaving. Cliff had been my photography lab instructor when he was a graduate student at Iowa State before joining John. At John Strohm, he was my supervisor and professional mentor. "You can't leave," Cliff announced. "You're too important to us. We need you to edit the *Top Farmers Intelligence* newsletter. Go home over the weekend and pray about it. I'll make an offer when you get back." When I came in on Monday, he said, "We're going to keep you here, Merrill, and give you a thirty thousand-dollar salary."

Well, at that point I'm saying to myself, Friday I was worth $12,000 — my salary at the time — and today I'm worth $30,000. I curbed a little flash of anger and turned it into something more creative. "I've already been led by the Lord to go back to Iowa," I said. "So we're not negotiating whether or not I'm leaving. The negotiation is if you want me do the newsletter from there." Cliff ended up hiring me do the newsletter for $24,000 a year. And just like that I went from being an employee to having a client. It was a leap of faith that turned out to be a very profitable thing to do. **Life tip #46: Never sell yourself too cheaply.**

• • •

I had worked for John for six and a half great, great years. Now it was time to strike out on my own. In October 1969, Carol and I loaded everything we owned into a rental truck and moved to Cedar Falls, Iowa, a town near the Oster farm and the place my paternal grandparents now lived. We rented a little house, took the money we'd made on our Woodstock house, bought another farm, the Allen farm, at $600 an acre and launched a publishing business with one employee—me!

Four

Professional Farmers of America
Leading Industry Change from Cedar Falls, Iowa

I've known his family as neighbors for years. That boy is going places.
—Mike Jepson, neighbor and member of
Professional Farmers of America

The Cedar Falls we returned to in 1969 was very different from the one I left in 1958. Back then, Main Street was the center of our lives once we left the Oster driveway. Saturdays were for shopping and chatting. The street was swarming with shoppers, moviegoers and socializers. In the 100 block, the Regent Theatre was crowded. In the mornings, the Regent Café was a great breakfast stop.

Across the street, Burt Multhoff's Tire Shop and the Purina Store were regular places for Dad to buy supplies and find good conversation. Mom, armed with coupons from the *Waterloo Courier*, moved between Diamond's Grocery and the A&P Grocers to find the best bargains. The dime store on Main Street, a regular stop for us kids, and Lyle's Barber Shop were humming in 1958.

Jim Walmsley's Coast to Coast store was bustling and competing with Western Auto, the other hardware store.

Two banks and the savings and loan were on or near Third and Main. Two implement dealers, a grain elevator and the L. L. Boxwell veterinary office at the corner of Third and State Streets where frequent stops as we walked the streets saying hello to friends and neighbors.

By 1969 supermarkets like Big T in Waterloo and Piggly Wiggly in Cedars Falls had wiped out Main Street grocers. Walmart, Kmart and Crossroads Shopping Center in Waterloo and College Square in Cedar Falls were putting pressure on the remaining retail businesses. "My customers can buy things cheaper at Kmart then I can buy them from my wholesaler," my friend Jim Walmsley of the Coast to Coast store told me.

Around this time, Cedar Falls lost two hardware stores, the Purina Store, Willoughby's Dry Goods and two shoe stores. Cedar Falls Main Street was being emptied. I had no idea in the fall of 1969 that my 10-by-30 office would grow to occupy 100,000 square feet of space and help provide stability and renewal of my hometown Main Street a few years later.

But let's get back to moving day, 1969. Friends lined the sidewalk as we unloaded our belongings into Goldy Baker's place, our rental for a few months. The next morning was one of the happiest moments in my life, along with the day Carol said she would marry me and the days our children were born. As I got out of bed and put my feet on the floor, I realized I worked for myself now. No boss. I didn't have to run to the office. After breakfast I jumped in my car and drove over and chatted with my dad. Then I went to my farm where Steve was working and had a chat with him. And then I went to my office at 126 Main Street in Cedar Falls, directly across the street from the Blackhawk Café and Hotel. It was a little rented space I had arranged for $70 a month.

My confidence to start my own business was boosted by

recalling a few one-liners from people who saw potential in me. When I was a college freshman, a neighbor, Vernon Schoeman, told me, "Knuckles, if you ever need an investor, count me in." (His son Paul had cleaned my clock on the school bus in a no-contest fistfight 10 years earlier. I'm glad that nickname never stuck!) And once as I stepped off a hotel elevator, I overheard my Iowa farming neighbor Mike Jepson say to a group of agribusiness leaders, "I've known his family as neighbors for years. That boy is going places."

John Strohm had also seen potential in me and taught me vital professional and personal lessons. Besides the lessons in journalism, I got to watch him start, run and sell various companies, including Top Farmers of America. I saw the whole process from finding an original idea to attracting money and the right people to going public and selling. It was an education I would build on with my own company. Most important in this life-changing move was the nudge from the Holy Spirit and Carol's validation that this seemed to be the Lord's will.

I launched Communication Consultants Inc. (ComCo) in October 1969. What I had to sell was my journalistic skill bundled with a mind that had been trained on the Oster farm, at John Strohm Associates and by personal experience trading commodity futures. I already had some clients lined up and quickly acquired others. The pitch I made to companies: take some of the budget you are spending on caps, pens and other handouts, and instead, provide your customers with decision-making information that will help them earn a profit.

Life tip #47: Start with a big, unique idea.

ComCo clients included the American Soybean Association, AmChem, MidAmerica Commodity Exchange, Central National Bank, Elanco, *Top Farmer Intelligence*,

AgriFinance magazine, *Successful Farming* magazine, *Banking* magazine and Hubbard Milling Company, among others. These publishing activities let me probe lots of new ideas, new technologies and new trends in farming. The Lord gave me favor in selling more business than I could deliver myself, so Darrell Jobman joined me part time in 1970 and full time later.

The American Soybean Association offered me a full time job just as we arrived in Cedar Falls, but I made a proposal instead, similar to what I had done with *Top Farmers*. "Why don't you let me do a newsletter aimed at the biggest soybean growers in America? And instead of giving them free information, we'll charge them fifty dollars a year. I'll do a revenue split with you."

They agreed and this turned out to be absolutely vital to our future success because it was a test run for what I wanted to do with Professional Farmers of America. I put out the first *Soybean Profit* newsletter in 1970. As I worked with ASA, headquartered in Hudson, a few miles away, I learned a lot from their head of direct marketing, Larry Krueger. He had a good handle on which name lists were the most profitable to use in agriculture. That information, combined with that acquired at the American Society of Agronomy and Top Farmers of America, became the gold mine for many future direct mail endeavors.

Life tip #48: Test your big idea.

I picked up another client around this time, AmChem Manufacturing. I produced the AmChem University, a day-long seminar for their customers in what was a precursor for the Pro Farmer Institute, a newsletter and several *Soybean Profit* publications. AmChem was based in Philadelphia. The Lord used trips to Pennsylvania to renew my relationship with Jerry Carlson. He worked in Philadelphia as the managing editor of *Farm Journal*, the nation's most prestigious farm magazine. Jerry was the best writer I knew. He expressed himself in writing far better than I did. I knew I needed him.

"Jerry, I've got an idea for an outfit called Professional Farmers of America," I told him on a visit in the spring of '72. "We could provide high-quality, timely marketing information in a newsletter to the top one percent of the nation's farmers who have annual gross incomes over one hundred thousand dollars." We would deliver it first class so many would receive it the next morning." I made pitches to him on my various trips trying to sell him on a big vision and coming to work in little Cedar Falls.

Jerry and his wife, Jill, finally came to Cedar Falls for a serious look. After driving them around town and giving them the hard sell, Jerry asked, "What would happen if I said no to this idea?" I said, "Well, very likely, there will never be a Professional Farmers of America." I was telling him how very important he was to me. Thankfully, he said yes and we started laying the groundwork for Professional Farmers that summer. He left *Farm Journal* in December and moved to Cedar Falls. He was a minority partner, but he had been my fraternity pledge father, so he had my respect. We always treated each other as equals. I never had an awkward conversation or battle with Jerry in all our years together. **Life tip #49: Attract the best talent available.**

• • •

I was flying home from Chicago in the fall of 1972 on a $66 Ozark airline ticket. Otis Budlong, a neighboring farmer was in the adjacent seat. He was on his way home from a National Cattle Feeders conference. Otie, as we called him, was a big cattle feeder.

I spelled out our plans for Professional Farmers of America, and without asking him, he forked over $50 to become Charter Member number one. His boys, Irv and Del, were just out of college doing entry-level financial transactions — Irv doing it for himself, Del for a California bank. In the next few years, Irv would partner with me in starting the *HomeTowner*, a shopper for Cedar Falls and Waterloo. Del would partner in Commodity Hedgers and Traders.

My entrepreneurial training started way back with my dad when he taught me how to make money with four pigs. It was advanced by John Strohm and accelerated by on-the-job experience with Top Farmers of America, the American Soybean Association and AmChem. These successes, and Jerry's extensive experience and presence, gave us the confidence to launch Professional Farmers of America, which defined our early business careers. It married our love of farming with our passion to make a difference through publishing ventures that helped framers profit by making better marketing decisions.

My work for *Ford Farming* and *Top Farmers* and Jerry's work for *Farm Journal* gave each of us opportunities to travel across America visiting farmers to learn how they made decisions, created wealth and fed the world. We knew their hearts and needs as well as anybody. Our knowledge of what they needed, particularly in the area of economic information, put us on the cutting edge. *Top Farmers* had a head start in reaching this audience, but they missed the mark. It was published monthly like a magazine, so it was not a newsletter. Top *Farmer Intelligence* didn't offer concrete buy-sell advice. The American Soybean Association newsletter I created, *Soybean Profits*, was more on target in terms of frequency and delivery, but it didn't deal with the futures market or give advice at the request of its executive director, Chet Randolph. The stage was set for the *Pro Farmer* newsletter.

Jerry and I dropped our first *Pro Farmer* direct mail package inviting 100,000 farmers to join in December 1972. It was a $40,000 investment that netted 1,000 charter members. This immediate success caused Top Farmers, my former employer and client, to threaten an injunction. I drove to Milwaukee and sat down with Cliff Ganschow and their lawyer, and I laid out my case. I knew our product was unique and different from Top Farmers and explained it to them. It was a very difficult session. I told them their lawsuit didn't have a chance. But I left thinking they might have a chance, and we might have gotten ourselves into a real mess.

Jerry and I talked about how an injunction would keep us from growing. We decided to drop a second mailing in the next 10 days in case we got shut down. I borrowed another $30,000 or $40,000, and we put another 100,000 invitations in the mail. The legal threat forced us to do two mailings instead of one. As a result, we doubled our number of paid subscribers to 2,000. That gave us the critical mass we needed to get through our first year.

Life tip #50: Don't be afraid of risk.

This was another situation where the invisible hand of God was at work, this time through a legal threat, which never materialized. I didn't talk to anyone at Top Farmers for several years afterward. Professional Farmers of America was growing to 32,000 members. Top Farmers of America was dying. Then, a decade later, I was speaking to a large group of agribusiness leaders at the American Farm Foundation meeting in Oakbrook, Illinois. John Strohm was in the audience. At the end of my speech, which drew a standing ovation, he got up and said, "That's my boy. I hired him out of college and made him what he is today." He gave me a big hug; the tension between our organizations was totally removed with his generous gesture.

The first issue of *Pro Farmer* newsletter went out in March 1973. We promised 32 newsletters during the year but decided to go weekly, giving our members more than they paid for.

Life tip #51: Exceed your clients' expectations.

That month we also did the first Pro Farmer seminars in Peoria and Des Moines. Whenever I talked to farmers, I did so as a fellow farmer. I had a farming operation as large or larger than many of our Pro Farmer members. We offered farmers discounts on chemicals, arranged through friend Dale Hassman, an idea that became so popular that chemical companies began selling directly to farmers themselves. We offered members Pro Farmer business cards and stationery and access to the best information sources Jerry and I could muster.

The success of Professional Farmers of America rested on the hiring of an outstanding team of leaders who had already proven themselves. Jerry and I hired the best people we could find to write for *Pro Farmer*, our flagship newsletter. We laid the tracks for the company, but the wave of talent the Lord put in our path over the next couple of years was nothing less than spectacular.

Darrell Jobman, our first full time associate, preceded Jerry by a few months. He had been the farm editor for the Waterloo Courier. He wrote a critical article on commodity futures that was filled with inaccuracies in my opinion. I wrote him a letter straightening out his bad understanding and told him about the positive role the futures market played in managing financial risk. That's how we got acquainted. I hired him part time in 1970, and two years later he came on full time just before Jerry Carlson joined to help launch *Pro Farmer*. His father-in-law wasn't sure he should make this decision, so I was asked to pay for a life insurance policy on me with Darrell as the beneficiary in case I died while he was working for me. Remember, at this time I had no track record.

Darrell was a quick learner about hedging risks. The life insurance policy was his hedge. I was hedging corn and hogs. Darrell was hedging me. He went on to become a legend in the futures industry. So far, he's not been able to cash in on that policy, if it even exists.

One of our early key hires was Rex Wilmore. We came out of college about the same time. I was from Iowa State, and Rex was from Oklahoma State. We met at an editors' meeting and became immediate friends. Both of us had lost our fathers the year before. Jerry had worked with Rex at *Farm Journal* and recruited him to direct some of the early activities of Pro Farmer, including being the managing editor, then editor, of the newsletter.

Rex became an absolute genius in setting up structure, training people and providing them with performance standards. Rex was one of my two key business operations advisors for all companies over a long period of time. The other was Merlyn Vandekrol, a contact of Jerry's we brought on a few years later.

Life tip #52: Build a strong team.

We taught farmers how to use commodity futures to inform good decision making, which involved understanding a technical piece of information called the basis. The basis is the difference between the price of crops in Chicago and the price being paid at the local elevator. "Look up and down the railroad tracks," I told farmers. "See all those huge storage facilities. They're owned by grain companies, but we farmers paid for them with our ignorance because we don't understand how to market our grain. If we learn to know when to sell in futures and when to sell in cash, we can pay for our own storage and control our own destiny."

This insight changed the way farmers did their selling. They began putting up grain bins all over America. We helped level the playing field with the largest grain companies in the world by giving farmers quality information and decision-making tools. This helped us keep the wealth in rural communities instead of being gobbled up by conglomerates. Our leadership attracted a dozen other individuals and small advisory services who competed with Pro Farmer but helped us reshape the way farmers sold grain and livestock.

Pro Farmer seminars taught farmers to think differently about their future. We gave them a bigger vision as to what their business could look like. I often heard farmers say, "Oh, I'm just a farmer. Anybody can be a farmer." We came along with the idea that you are a professional and you need to learn professional techniques in some areas. Let us help you. In the process, we changed the mindset of our members from seeing farming as a way of life to one of treating it like a business. There's a statement I must have repeated hundreds of times in our seminars, "If you treat your farm like a way of life, it'll be a nice way of life. But if you treat it like a business, you might retire well."

Life tip #53: Deliver a unique message.

I loved to punctuate seminars with homespun farm boy humor. "You want to know my single biggest management mistake last year?" I would ask. "My Gleaner combine caught fire. My biggest mistake? I put it out." The crowds would roar because farmers were proud of their machinery brands, and most of them would have been driving John Deere or International Harvester products, so my follow-up line got another roar. "That Gleaner threw so much corn out the back we called her our Silver Seeder!"

The executives at Gleaner's Allis Chalmers headquarters in Milwaukee didn't give me the same roar. I got a strongly worded letter from their legal department warning me to stop telling jokes deprecating their brand, or they would sue me. I called the guy who wrote the letter and told him, "Go ahead and sue me, sir. And I will drive my combine to your Milwaukee headquarters and light a match to it, creating an even bigger PR mess. But as an alternative, why don't you just fix my darned combine?" The next week two men and a truck from headquarters showed up, completely gutted the combine and replaced nearly every moving part. I got a newly renovated combine, and the company avoided a public relations disaster of major proportions!

My next combine was a John Deere.

After a long, lonesome fall riding the tractor or combine, our members were ready for a time of fellowship with other leaders in their field. Late fall seminars drew a good following, but January through mid-March was the sweet spot. Seminars provided a good opportunity for our staff to be shoulder to shoulder with our members. Along with information on price outlook and land buying, we entertained attendees with positive mental attitude speakers — men like Louis Timberlake and Joe Batten, whose optimism came from their faith in God. We ran a first-class operation in stark contrast to the smoke-filled meeting rooms and disorganized meetings of the time. We started and finished in time. We didn't allow smoking or dirty jokes from the platform.

Well, almost never. At one Pro Farmer seminar in Des Moines, I noticed Jimmy Dean checking into the airport hotel. I invited him to say a few words. He had the audience laughing at his smut, but after I dragged him off the platform, I apologized for my mistake and the off-color interruption.

Our members came to seminars to expand their knowledge. But we also tried to make them feel good about themselves and their farming profession, no matter how small their farm. This story I told on a hundred or more platforms always served a purpose: "A Texan stops at an Iowa farm and asks the farmer, "How much land you own?" The farmer replies, 'Well, it runs along this road here to that creek down there and up along that fence line, about ninety acres.'"

"Well," says the Texan, "I have so much land that it takes me from breakfast to lunch to drive around it." "Yep," says the Iowa farmer. "Had a car like that once myself."

Farm kids sometimes came to school with a certain air about them. Just before leaving for school, we might be asked to turn off a faucet in the hog house or make a last-minute stop in the dairy barn. Such stops made a daylong impression, a slight farm aroma. So this story had a ring of truth to it and always got a good laugh: This farmer, after selling a load of hogs, stops at a local coffee shop. Three guys on motorcycles pull in and sit next to him with an eye to picking a fight. One guy says, "Do you smell a pigpen in here?" Another bumps into the farmer and calls him a hick. The farmer leaves quietly, and the biker says to the cashier, "That farmer isn't much of a man. He wouldn't even defend himself when we insulted him." "Nope," says the waiter. "And he's not much of a driver, either. He just backed his truck over three motorcycles."

I would include a few paragraphs in each of my speeches about my spiritual optimism concerning the future of agriculture or the future of business. I would say that I'm an optimist because I've read the last chapter of the Book. I know how things are going to turn out. I talked openly about the faith of our founding fathers and my personal faith in Jesus Christ as my ultimate reason to be optimistic.

Our members of Professional Farmers of America were more than customers. Many of them felt they belonged to a family. We laughed with them. We cried with them. They knew that when the economy pinched them, it pinched our staff, too.

Carol traveled with me and was by my side at many of our events. So much so that she became known as Mrs. Pro Farmer. The staff often gathered for dessert after our meetings and seminars, and Carol brought bags of shredded coconuts. She had noticed that this ingredient was missing in restaurant ice cream sundaes, and so she provided it. The company had a family feel. We made our recreational vehicle and vacation properties available to senior management, and we would often be together as families. Carol and the kids helped create the family atmosphere that was part of the Oster culture. I couldn't have done what I've done in business and ministry over the years without her love and solid support.

Professional Farmers of America introduced ideas that were different from what was being taught in universities. University outlook information was usually based on a single economist who talked about the outlook for cattle, hogs, corn, soybeans, whatever. But we interviewed the best economists in America, synthesized their ideas and combined them with our technical analysis. This approach ruffled a lot of feathers. Our critics said, "You're just a bunch of writers." My response was, "Yes, we're writers, but we're smart people and we all grew up on the farm. I would rather hire a good journalist and teach him or her how to gather and synthesize economic advice than hire an economist and try to teach him how to write and speak plain English!"

Farmers were accustomed to getting outlook information through their college extension services. The information was published in newspapers and magazines while farm broadcasters delivered snippets by radio. The *Pro Farmer* newsletter arrived by first-class mail, included market analysis that considered what the best of the state economists could offer, plus the exclusive *Pro Farmer* sources including our own staff reporters and took into account a technical analysis. This triangulated approach may have been my original idea, but key leaders on our team perfected it.

Others noted our unique value. Loren Kruse, Editor of *Successful Farming*, once said, "I decided long ago to skim the bulk of my mail, but to always read *Pro Farmer*. If it isn't in *Pro Farmer*, it probably isn't worth knowing."

We also had consulting experts who helped us pick up on what was coming, so our advice positioned farmers to adjust accordingly. There was Bob Fisher. Bob was another of the mentors God sent to me at key moments. He helped us understand and forecast the long-term impact of President Nixon taking the US off the gold standard on August 15, 1971. I was already buying all the land I could when Bob said, "This is a new ball game, Merrill. The value of hard assets is heading higher." I bought a Grundy County farm for $500 that fall and sold it in 2000 for $5,000 an acre.

Fred Breth was our Russia Watcher. He tipped us off on the blockbuster grain purchase that contributed to skyrocketing prices in 1973. That was the summer of the great Russian Grain Robbery. It was called that because the Russians bought so much grain, mostly wheat, that it caused the price of all grains to almost double over the next year.
Life tip #54: Get insights from your peers.

I was becoming known and respected by experts — men like Conrad Leslie, Jr. — in the commodity futures market. Leslie was a legend in the agribusiness community. His preopening morning market newsletter and his monthly crop estimates of American corn, soybeans and wheat production were read and studied around the world. The *New York Times* called him "the nation's leading private harvest forecaster." Leslie was a longtime confidant, informer and friend of Pro Farmer and a seminar speaker.

I can still remember exactly where I was standing when I got my first call from Conrad "Les" Leslie. I took it on a wall phone, which tells you how long ago that was — 1973. Les had been given my name by the American Soybean Association, one of my clients at the time. He wanted information on the corn blight, and they told him I had been traveling around the country taking pictures and analyzing the situation. "Merrill Oster's your man," they told him.

We became friends, and Conrad eventually became a client of Pro Farmer, FutureSource and Oster Dow Jones Commodity News. I made frequent visits to his Chicago office. I opened a trading account and became his customer. His career lasted 50 years. He was a member of the Chicago Board of Trade for more than 40 years. Les passed away on Christmas Day, 2018, at the age of 95. He had sent me his final market tip just a few weeks before he died.

• • •

At Professional Farmers, we not only knew how to create a unique editorial product under Jerry Carlson's leadership, but we also knew how to sell it. Jerry and I wrote the first direct mail piece based on experiences he had picked up at *Farm Journal* and those I had with the *Soybean Profits* newsletter and other publications. Rex Wilmore soon soaked up all our knowledge and with the help of consultant Dick Benson became the best direct mail writer in the company. Even outside consultants like Benson could not match the results we got from Rex's letters.

We sold everything we created — newsletters, magazines,

seminars, books — using direct mail. We rented name lists from magazine companies like Farm Industry News, Soybean Digest and Successful Farming. We kept track of every offer we made, so we knew which offer worked for which list. We tested various appeals by doing split runs. A mailing of 100,000 may have tested six to 10 different ideas. Comparing one headline on the envelope with another, one lead paragraph with another, short letters with longer ones.

Our database of what worked and what didn't work was on paper and in our heads. Over time, we knew what appeals, what keywords and phrases were most likely to get results of more than 0.5 percent. A gangbuster result, a 1 percent return, would be rarely achieved. We moved beyond gut feel on what worked in the early days to making databased decisions. The key was test, test, test!

Life tip #55: Test, test, test!

Although I had accumulated a good deal of direct mail experience, I headed to the Direct Mail Marketing Association to look for the best consultant in the industry. The same name came up in the first three conversations I had, so I walked to the host hotel registration desk and asked for Dick Benson. He agreed to come to the lobby and look at our recent direct mail promotions for membership in Professional Farmers of America.

"That's pretty crappy stuff, but I think I can help you. It will be three thousand dollars per day plus expenses." I never blinked. Benson showed up at the Waterloo airport two weeks later. As he reached the top of the long, creaky stairway to our second-floor offices, he said, "I can see you can't afford me, but if you ever need me in the future, you're coming to my office in Amelia Island, Florida."

In the next couple of hours after pouring over our

mailing results and spectacular renewal rate of over 90 percent, he whipped out a whopper — worth $50,000 in the next year. "You guys could afford to spend thirty dollars for a sign-up premium, given your high renewal rate. You are in the renewal business. Spend what you need to get them in the door!"

Rex found a RadioShack handheld calculator for $35 or $40. It was so popular as a new member premium that we became the biggest buyer of handheld calculators in the world. For the next four years, we doubled our membership every year until we peaked at 32,000.

Rex and I used Dick Benson as a direct mail strategist for several years by spending two days at his Amelia Island home picking his brain. We had tapped into the mother lode of experience that propelled every new product and service we launched.

Life tip #56: Pay up for the best advice.

We also conducted travel seminars for our farmer members. In 1979 I led the first delegation of American members of Professional Farmers of America to be openly welcomed in China. There on the Malu People's Commune on the outskirts of Shanghai, I discovered China's latent power. The leader of the commune beckoned me to the window of his conference room where we could see farmland for a mile or more. He explained that all the land out there belonged to the commune. Then with a twinkle in his eye and a twitch of his finger outlining a small piece of land, he grinned and said through the interpreter, "That's mine."

The power of the right to own private poverty is implied and embedded in the commandment "Thou shalt not steal." The world was about to see that power unleashed. Within three years China was producing more food from private plots than from communes, stirring the sleeping giant into a frenzy of growth.

This glimpse into China made our staff aware of the country's impact on the world as their growing appetite for meat made them big customers for our soybeans. Of course, this impacted the price of the commodity and its underlying asset, the farmland I loved to talk about, improve, own and just generally enjoy.

My international travel had actually begun in 1961 when the Iowa State Traveling Aggies bus made a 3,500-mile swing around America, southern Canada and northern Mexico as part of a course that completed my bachelor's degree. At 21, my agricultural eyes were opened to the problems and opportunities of cattle ranching, vegetable farming, cotton growing and mining—all experiences outside of anything one could observe in Iowa.

My subsequent adventures over thousands of miles of the earth's surface convinced me that the land lying between the Missouri and Ohio rivers was the best place in the world to make a safe long-term investment. It still is. My early travels had an agricultural twist as I searched for land price implications. My later travel was aimed at filling the financial information needs of global customers. And finally, my ministry travel was aimed at advancing the gospel around the world. I'm a million-miler on United. The Lord only knows how many miles I logged on Pan Am, TWA, Ozark and a host of others.

By the end of the 1970s, 32,000 high-income farmers and agribusinessmen relied on *Pro Farmer* and our other newsletters and seminars for market data and buy-sell advice. We wound up influencing the people who controlled more than 50 percent of America's annual agricultural income.

Internally we communicated a set of values that created

a unique culture. Eventually we put together a handbook with the vision and mission statements of the company. In it we outlined the values and principles by which we operated. We didn't call them biblical principles, but they came straight out of the Bible. Our mission was "to serve God by nurturing our people, to help our customers manage financial risk, to build a solid global information services company, to pursue excellence in everything we do."

Some of these ideas were influenced by Bill Pollard who was the CEO of ServiceMaster at a time when it was a Fortune 100 company with about 250,000 employees worldwide. We served together on the board of Emmaus Bible College in Chicago and got acquainted. I knew that ServiceMaster had this wonderful corporate culture, so I invited myself to Bill's office one day and we talked through their culture. Their corporate objectives were "to honor God in all we do, to help people develop, to pursue excellence, to grow profitably."

Our core values expressed what I personally believed and tried to live out:

We are created with a purpose.
We grow by exercising our unique gifts.
We are part of a team.
We are individually responsible.
The truth sets us free.
Selflessness frees us to serve.
Love goes beyond fairness.
Occasional pruning promotes new growth.
Excellence adds distinctive value.
Wealth creators serve society.
Forgiveness erases mistakes.
Optimism hastens growth.

Life tip #57: Shared values create a strong culture.

I didn't hammer on my Christian faith, but it informed everything I did and was the basis for my optimism. Merlyn Vandekrol shared my faith and my optimism. He was the son of a pastor, and he became one of our outstanding managers and sort of an internal pastor. He had the ability to listen well. He had more patience than I had. People would open up to Merlyn because of his godly demeanor. He advanced the cause of Christ through lovingly managing people and handling many difficult personnel problems. He hosted Bible studies in the company. I stayed out of them because I didn't want to be seen as pressuring people to be in a Bible study, but I certainly supported them. We worked side by side until colon cancer took his life. His death was a huge loss to me and everyone else who knew him.

Years earlier I had learned a great management lesson from Steve Shoemaker, my farm manager. One day, while I was giving him specific instructions on which field to go to next and how much time to spend on each project, he just stood by the gate gazing out over the field and shuffling his feet. I could see he was deciding if he should say what was really on his mind. Then he said, "Merrill, if you would just tell me what you want to accomplish and then let me decide how to accomplish it, I would feel a lot less nervous, and you would have a lot more time to be at your desk in Cedar Falls."

Wow. This from a high school graduate several years my junior. That comment influenced the way I handled my working relationship with business associates ever since.

I entrusted large chunks of responsibility to Steve, Rex and Merlyn. As we matured, pretty much everybody else in the organization reported to them, but I still ran staff meetings and the brainstorming sessions we had on Mondays. Management-level people gathered at Bishop's Buffet where we discussed what they were picking up in the marketplace. I always challenged them, "Don't mess around with small thinking. Let's see if we can discover a million-dollar idea. What's a new product or a service idea that would generate a million dollars of new revenue?"

Life tip #58: Expect unique contributions.

When I hired people, I would frequently say to them, "This is your job description right now, but if you're doing exactly the same thing 12 months from now, we've hired wrong. Get on top of what you're asked to do and then look for opportunities to grow. Keep one eye on what's going on in the company and the other on our marketplace."

I never hesitated to fire someone after making a few tries to find a fit, but I usually did it delicately. We had an artist who did beautiful illustrations but could not crank out enough volume of the more basic stuff like page layouts to be worth his salary. I called him into my office, told him how talented he was, but that his particular talent would probably have to find another home to be fully utilized.

"I'm not sure, but have I just been fired?" he questioned.

"Oh no," I replied. "I'm just saying in the next month or so you should look for a better place to do the things you do best." He was a talented guy. He smiled knowingly and found other work in a month.

One time we had an alcoholic working for us in Chicago who got really ticked off when we fired him for poor performance. He knew a Christmas party was coming up. He called me and said he would be there, uninvited and with a gun. I hired a bodyguard and kept my eye on the door all night. Nothing happened, thank the Lord.

• • •

I never had an official mentoring program, but many of the people who say I mentored them were at my elbow day after day. They could read my eyeballs, they could hear my telephone conversations. We had lots of conversation in the hallways or standing in the doorways of our offices. We were learning on the run. Later on when we began to sell companies, some of these guys took the transition as an opportunity to launch their own businesses. More than 20 former Oster executives started their own companies and did quite well. But not all.

I hired Russ Wassendorf when he was working at the American Soybean Association. He quickly learned the basics of futures trading by serving our customers in various capacities. He left our company to start his own. But he unfortunately went on to use his industry knowledge to serve himself. Today Russ sits in a federal prison in Terre Haute, Indiana. He started a brokerage firm that held customer cash reserves used as trading equity. Russ dipped into his customers' cash for his own personal use and covered it up with clever document falsifications that fooled regulators for years. When federal authorities caught on to the theft, Russ was convicted and put away, probably for life. We all hurt for Russ and pray for a repentant spirit and a return to God.

There were a few misappropriations of position and power that led to my firing talented men. I caught one executive negotiating a sale of my company that included an ownership package for himself without my knowledge. When I learned of this, I listened to his pitiful explanation before walking him to his car to retrieve his company credit card and door key. Another sold information from our company and had the check mailed to his home. When I verified that, I gave him a call and invited him to stay home — forever.

In my 50-plus years of business ownership, these disappointments represent a tiny minority of people. I have been blessed to have been surrounded by men and women who were hard working, talented and totally trustworthy.

I've already mentioned Jerry Carlson, Darrell Jobman, Merlyn Vandekrol and Rex Wilmore. Because our early success created the need for list management and circulation management, Rex hired Ann Davis, whose outspoken leadership skills kept our growing pains in proper perspective. Mike Rodby, a software genius, created our first computerized accounting software, then became our go-to guru on all things software. His quiet, just-get-it-done demeanor made him an internal hero.

Larry Graham was a well-respected former *Prairie Farmer* editor and executive director of the Illinois Pork Producers before he joined Professional Farmers of America. Although we intended to hire Larry as editor of our *PorkPro* newsletter, the seminar business was becoming so successful that he became the head of the Pro Farmer Institute, organizing up to 25 seminars a year around the country for our members. We typically attracted 75 to 200 people from more than 20 states at each of the seminars.

Mike Walsten joined us as editor of the *PorkPro* newsletter and went on to head up other activities including the startup of our Futures World News organization that put 25 journalists at work gathering market sensitive information that was used by all of our companies and resold to many commercial clients, including commodity traders.

Lee Searle, a great economic intellect with a good pen, was *Pro Farmer* editor behind Jerry and Rex. When Lee's father offered him a partnership in the home farm, they came to my office looking for approval. What could I say? A chance to be an owner of a large hog farm? Better jump.

Ron Michaelson took over after Lee until we found an ever better position for Ron. He went from editor of *Pro Farmer* to leader of our Pro Farmer audio service lining up radio stations around the country to carry our *Pro Farmer* report. Bob Coffman was field editor at *Farm Journal* when we hired him. He became a prolific writer on a wide range of topics.

Kathleen Tanzy was a quick learning journalist who started in Cedar Falls but quickly became a Washington and New York reporter for us. Susan Abbott stepped up to become an effective *Futures* magazine reporter. Susan Bolt set big goals for herself and achieved them as she moved from putting lines on price charts, working for Karla Kelley, to moving on to our Washington office to earn White House press credentials.

The *Pro Farmer* newsletter, a name coined by Jerry Carlson, was our flagship. Jerry was the first editor, followed by Rex Wilmore, Lee Searle, Ron Michaelson and then Dan Manternach. We hired Dan off a hog farm. We saw something in this guy that was special. He started as a writer for *Pro Farmer* and became the editor. He went on to become the president of Professional Farmers of America. He had a good handle on every aspect of the business. He was also able to step into my role accepting speaking engagements on behalf of the organization. This freed me up to focus on fighting financial fires, expanding other enterprises and finding new ways to serve the Lord in ministry activities.

Jim Wiesemeyer could squeeze out market-sensitive news from his Washington, D.C., sources almost daily. Scott Rogers and Wendy Speckerman took the Pro Farmer Institute through the farm crisis of the 1980s by inventing new topics that provided needed counsel at the time. John Jokerst led the charge with Mark Wooderson as we created new ways to deliver information electronically. Paul Wilcox, Glen Ring and Karla Kelly learned charting and technical analysis and delivered quality editorial material that made all of our publications unique.

Terry Wooten had a knack for finding market-moving stories and for training young editors to do likewise. Elizabeth Curry supported Jerry on the *Landowner* newsletter and coauthored our book on land buying. Pete Cornell as art department head touched every editorial product and sales piece in one way or another. Ginger Sczala was able to get interviews with leading traders and industry leaders and always found a good human-interest twist to the many get-rich-quick stories.

As we grew, Len Swiatley headed our in-house prepress operation that gave us the quickest turnaround time in the industry. To lower our costs, Len put two salespeople on the road selling our services to clients across Iowa. Sandy Golz and Sandy Hyde were my executive assistants during the fastest years of our growth. These highly talented women both went on to serve in management roles, Sandy Golz as our company production manager and Sandy Hyde as a vice president of Winnebago Industries. Rex's assistant, the late Roberta Spring, could handle anything he put on her desk. Loris Prostine was one of my first executive assistants. She served in many support roles over the years with her sweet spirit, can-do attitude and fast fingers on the electric typewriter.

Chris Crane came to work for us for a year before going out on his own. Several of his friends thought his purchase of Comps was a bad idea, but I encouraged him to buy the business he was considering. "You need to do these five things if you want to turn the business around," I told him. He did all five of them and repositioned his company, Comps, for a multimillion-dollar sale.

This launched him into a career as a leader in Christian service organizations. He became CEO of Opportunity International. Opportunity provides microfinance services and transformational training to people in need to empower them to work their way out of chronic poverty in third-world countries. His leadership skills and fundraising expertise helped raise investment capital. Chris left Opportunity to start another international ministry called Edify. Edify assists entrepreneurs who offer quality Christ-centered education to children in underserved international communities.

Now at this stage in my life, I can see the fruit of the small investment I made in some very smart people like Chris who are now making a big difference in the world. Chris introduced me to Steve James. Steve has done some spectacular things in the world of business for me and in the world at large. He led the negotiations in our sale of Professional Farmers of America to *Farm Journal*, Oster Dow Jones Commodity News to Dow Jones and *Futures* magazine to a hedge fund. Although Steve and Chris say I have mentored them, they have been conduits of God's grace to me as a businessman and Christian peer.

Life tip #59: We need each other.

Five

Buying, Selling, Building Equity
Leveraging Land and Commodities

Merrill, you were there when it all started.
— Leo Melamed, chairman, Chicago Mercantile Exchange

One of the great things about America and the free enterprise system is that a guy with almost nothing has a chance to make it big. One popular way is to take the little you have and leverage it. The ultimate leverage opportunity is the futures market, where with $1,000 you control $20,000 worth of grain in 1960. Commodity futures trading was not viewed in a positive way by most agricultural colleges in the 1960s, but I took a serious interest in it and took verbal opposition to the traditional university viewpoints. I was 23 years old, had a graduate degree in agricultural journalism and very little cash, but I wanted to see if I could make trading work for me.

I began trading 1,000 bushel lots of corn priced around $1 per bushel. Talking to farmers had given me the idea that corn was going higher. I made some money, but more important, I got to thinking seriously about futures as a risk-management tool. My local stock broker, Virgil Smith, operated out of his house two doors down from our house in Woodstock. He showed me how he used price charts to spot price trends. Lessons we learned together laid important building blocks under each of our businesses.

I visited the Chicago Mercantile Exchange after reading an article in the *Wall Street Journal* about Sydney Maduff and his successful egg and pork-belly trading. I called him with some questions and wound up becoming his client. He helped me learn how to take risks and how not to by trading pork bellies. He watched me blow out my account with a limit-down speculative loss of $2,400 in pork bellies when my net worth was about $2,400 in 1964. I was technically broke but better educated. Being broke is only a temporary inconvenience in the eyes of an entrepreneur.
Life tip #60: Take only risks you can afford.

I visited the Chicago Open Board of Trade where I noticed a guy drawing lines on a chart. He would make a trade, sit there and draw another bar. When the trading day ended, I noticed he drove off in a new Mercedes. It struck me that this guy must know something. I came back the next day and sat next to him and we talked between trades. He gave me a breakthrough vision on how to use trend lines on commodity price charts as a timing tool to decide when to buy and sell. A few years later, I would pass along that tool through Professional Farmers of America, Commodity Price Charts and FutureSource.

The concept that intrigued me the most was how the commodity futures market could be harnessed by farmers to manage their financial risk. I understood futures markets well enough to use it in my own farming operation. I learned that through pricing my hogs by selling a futures contract and buying a corn contract and a soybean meal contract,

I could lock in a price relationship that greatly reduced my risk. In fact, by hedging I was able to double the size of my operation with no more total financial risk than a neighboring farmer half my size.

Grasp that. When the Lord revealed this truth to me, it gave our companies a unique angle to use in helping our Pro Farmer members. And it helped me grow our businesses by personally investing in more appreciating farmland while carefully managing our risk.

Armed with that reduced operational risk, I could justify owning twice as much land. I loved to buy land. I was never greedy. I just wanted to own the farm that adjoined me. Get it? Our seminar attendees sure did.

Life tip #61: Manage your risk with futures.

I began to write and speak about hedging crops and buying more land, not from an academic point of view but as a fellow farmer who had his own money on the line. That real-life stuff really appealed to Professional Farmers of America members who attended our land buying seminars. What I learned in the school of hard knocks I passed along and helped thousands of investors make better risk management decisions. This hands-on knowledge became a core component of nearly all of our products and services at Professional Farmers of America.

Irv Budlong, whom I mentioned in Chapter 4, was buying farms and selling them to Chicago investors. We took a trip to Minnesota to look at some farms for sale. We decided to buy a 300-acre Minnesota farm together. A year later Irv stepped into the doorway of my office and said, "Half of this farm is too small a deal for either of us. Why don't I name a price, and you say buy or sell? One of us will own the whole thing." I accepted the challenge. He named the price. I said, "Sold!" Irv's face flushed. He obviously stepped in to sell me a farm. He had only seen me in buy mode. Now he owned the farm.

We had a similar exchange while vacationing with our families on Waikiki, Hawaii, some years later. Neither of us had done a deal for nearly a week, so he concocted one while wading in the water. We jointly owned the *HomeTowner*, a growing shopper that was losing $50,000 a year. But it had potential because there were buyers looking for such properties.

"How about one of us pick a price, and the other can either buy or sell?" Irv said.

"OK, shoot me a number," I challenged as our wives bathed in the warm sun.

"Fifty thousand," Irv blurted.

I took two more steps and felt totally confident in my response, "Sold!" Again, I saw the same little flush in Irv's face. I knew he would rather buy than sell. I now owned the *HomeTowner*. Later I added the *Cedar Falls Citizen*, and when the crisis of the early 1980s hit, I dumped the property for $250,000.

Life tip #62: Always be ready to buy or sell.

Commodity Hedgers and Traders was a brokerage firm that operated on the first floor under the Pro Farmer offices. I told Del Budlong I would be a financial partner but could not be distracted from my Pro Farmer responsibilities. Until Del walked into my office one day and said one of our brokers made a $25,000 mistake. Del lacked the money to cover his share. I made an immediate decision, without prayer or consultation with anyone, to pay for the loss and give Del my share of the company. I learned on that deal that if you are going to be at risk, you'd better be in control.

Life tip #63: Cut your losses short.

Another lesson I passed on from my own experience was how to use leverage to acquire farmland using small down payments and nonrecourse loans. I conducted a seven-hour seminar on land buying based largely on my own experiences, including examples of actual deals I had made. I've had many farmers tell me, "You saved my family farm because I bought additional farmland using the techniques you were teaching."

I shared my failures and successes. At one point I paid $3,000 an acre for a near-perfect 160-acre farm between Dike and New Hartford in 1982, only to see its value drop to $900 an acre in 1984. I let that farm go back to the previous owner, losing my 15 percent down payment. Several months later a local banker told me of a farm bordering my own that had gone into bankruptcy. I was able to get that for $900 an acre. So the farm I lost three miles away was replaced by one next door at the same price, but under improving economic conditions. God turned my setback into one of thanksgiving.

During the recession of 1982–85 in agriculture, I wanted to let a farm near Cedar Falls go back to its owner, Mack Gable, father of wrestling legend Dan Gable. Mack said, "I don't want the darned farm back, Merrill. Tell me what you can afford." God sent this generous, kind man into my life when I needed a break. We cut a deal I could afford, and it had nothing to do with my well-developed land negotiating skills. It was the grace of God. Mack was God's conduit of grace to me. That farm became a cornerstone piece of land for our Pinnacle Prairie 720-acre real estate development in Cedar Falls.

One of the most common questions I was asked when giving land-buying seminars was "It's easy for you to tell us about this, Mr. Oster. You've already bought ten farms. But how do you get your first farm?" And I would tell them what I told Jerry when we started Pro Farmer: It's not how much money you have that counts; it's where you can put it at the right time that makes the difference. I had put a small amount of money into a house, then rolled the profit into a piece of land, and then a small building in Cedar Falls, parlaying it from one thing to the next using financial leverage.

I was introduced to the leverage concept by Bill Morris, a professor at Purdue University. John Strohm had sent me to interview him for a farm story. He was buying houses for $1,000 down, painting them and increasing the rent to raise their value. Then he would put the higher value on his net worth statement and take that to the bank to borrow $3,000 to buy three more houses. He then moved into apartments and became a major real estate player in Indiana.

When he explained that to me, my jaw just dropped. I hadn't taken any economic classes where I could have learned about this. Instead, I learned it in this very practical on-the-job training. So I began buying farmland in 1967. My first purchase was an 80-acre farm I bought with 15 percent down and a 7 percent interest contract over 15 years. Those 80 acres and the 30 sows I bought were the forerunner to what grew at its peak to about 6,500 acres and a hog operation that farrowed and finished 28,000 hogs a year.

Many times I bought land by going to a farmer's kitchen table and saying, "I'd like to buy your farm. I don't have a lot of money, but I can give you a steady return. I'll give you ten percent down and the rest over ten years at six percent interest with a balloon at the end." I bought a lot of land on that basis.

Life tip #64: Use leverage wisely.

I've always been a bit of a horse trader. That's something that goes back to standing at the edge of the barnyard listening to my dad talk to a cattle buyer. The cattle buyer says, "I'll give you $24.75 for those cattle right now." Dad would just kick the dirt and say, "Well, I'm just going to think about that a little bit. There's another buyer coming in tomorrow." The buyer then says, "Oh, I'll give you $25." Dad says, "Okay, I'll do that." I learned about negotiating by watching my dad representing his own best interest against people who were exercising their own best interest. I'm so thankful for many of these magic moments when just watching my dad set the tone for the rest of my life.

When I share stories like this with other farm guys who had similar backgrounds, they say, "You received some lessons I never got." I believe that's because the Lord puts in us a sorting system that makes us particularly sensitive to the big plan he has for us. It's the Holy Spirit. Some have him; some don't. The Spirit was certainly at work in the next high-leverage investment I was about to make.

Six

Futures Magazine, FutureSource, Oster Dow Jones
Going Global with Futures

I made hundreds of investments last year,
and subscribing to Futures *was by far the best of them.*
— Isaac Etessami

My comfort with financial leverage and the success of Professional Farmers of America opened doors to other opportunities. In the fall of 1975, the Lord led me to one of the key purchases of my life. I was at an Agricultural Editors meeting in Chicago where I overheard a conversation at a table behind me that suggested *Commodities* magazine could be for sale. I walked to the lobby and called Todd Lofton, the founder of the magazine, and said, "Any chance your magazine might be for sale?" He said, "No, but where could I come and talk to you about it?"

He flew to Peoria, Illinois, to talk. I was speaking there at a Pro Farmer seminar. I wound up buying the magazine the same way I had been buying land—10 to 20 percent down with the balance paid over 10 years at 6 percent interest. Buying the magazine wasn't due to my brilliant planning; it was another piece of divine timing. The Lord put me in the right place at the right time with the right mindset. Problem: I negotiated a $50,000 down payment, but didn't have all the money lined up yet. I told my lawyer, Lewis Beecher, who said, "Come to my bank. Bill Rickert will loan you the fifty thousand." What a godsend! We ended up buying *Futures* with totally borrowed money. That's the ultimate in leveraging and risk. It's rarely a good business practice. By the grace of God, it worked this time.

After we bought the magazine our team began to cross-sell. We offered everything we had available through *Pro Farmer* to the subscribers of *Commodities*. We grew the magazine from a circulation of about 3,000 to 65,000. It went from a relatively small domestic publication to an international "spokes-publication" for the commodities industry for many years.

When we added *Commodities* to our portfolio of companies, advertisements with tear-out cards drove another wave of sales. In addition to our paid subscribers, we sent the magazine free to the best lists we could find in the industry, asking these prospects to subscribe to the magazine, and offering a host of our products on our advertising pages. Many companies found that advertising in the magazine was the only marketing program they needed. We created the highest direct response vehicle in the industry, hands down.

We became leaders in the fledgling hedging industry. Small brokerage offices were opening up in cities and towns all over America, hoping to cash in on the $40 per round-turn commissions created by each trade. New traders were flowing into the industry in the 1970s and 1980s as we legitimized commodity trading through our high-quality editorial materials in *Pro Farmer, Futures* magazine and other publications. We recommended that users of all commodities, currencies and financial products learn how to hedge. Hedging became a new word in the vocabulary of businessmen worldwide by the 1980s.

In 1983 we changed the name to *Futures* magazine. Darrell Jobman led us on the editorial side through the early years. Jerry Becker became our first full time salesperson. Advertising sales skyrocketed under his leadership. Ginger Szala later edited *Futures,* and Joe Bernardo as CEO shaped the company for sale. Bernardo was another one of those godsends. His management skills were just what we needed at that time. Of all my business associates, he was the only one who could run a marathon with me. He beat me by two seconds in the New York Marathon.

Out of that magazine we began to develop subsets. We launched Commodity Price Charts sold as an independent product. We sold seminars. People came to our Commodities Institute seminars just as they came to Pro Farmer seminars in large numbers and from many states. Author Larry Williams was an occasional speaker who could help us draw 200 to 250 paying customers to an all-day seminar.

We introduced so many people to the commodity futures industry that one of its founders, Leo Melamed, former chairman of the Chicago Mercantile Exchange. He once signed a book for me with the inscription:

"To Merrill,
You were there at the beginning and helped change the
destiny of futures.
With affection."

We used to do seminars together around the country. He and others have given me credit for being one of the forces that created the modern commodity futures industry as a risk management tool. I get the credit for the work of a large team of highly talented associates who helped us create and deliver one product after another.

Life tip #65: Leverage sales by cross selling.

I served two industries in my career: agriculture and futures trading. There was an overwhelming attitude of service to others in agriculture and a significant element of self-interest and greed in futures. At Oster, we sought to bring an attitude of service to both sectors.

Futures magazine and the various newsletters we were doing caused us to have need for news and data services. A company, Commodity Communications Corporation (CCC), came up for sale in 1981. I thought the owner, Bob Bishop, had his company way overpriced. "I don't have anywhere near that kind of money," I told him, "but I own a lot of farmland. I'll trade you a portfolio of farms plus some cash for your company." And he said, "I've always wanted to be in farming." So we cut a deal. I overpriced my farmland; he overpriced his company.

It seemed like a good deal for both parties at the time. The owner of CCC could get out of a company that required a significant infusion of cash for new technology. I converted farmland far from my Cedar Falls base into a company that opened up a new array of information products and services. Unloading 6,000 acres of highly leveraged farmland just before a price bust in 1981 turned out to be one of my most astute moves. I got out near the top in 1981 before the bottom fell out in farmland, but it was only by the grace of God.

CCC was headed by Russ Warner, the seller's brother-in-law when we acquired the company. We replaced him by bringing in Pete Fox, who headed the California sales office. Pete was an enthusiastic sales leader, a great Christian businessman with a big heart and great faith. When our lead salesman had a heart attack at a restaurant, Pete loaded him in his car and on the way to the hospital prayed, "Lord, save my friend Bill. After the job you did with Lazarus, this should be a piece of cake!" The Lord answered Pete's prayer. Bill lived. But a few weeks later, Pete bent over to untie his shoes after a morning run and died instantly of a heart attack himself.

The Lord used Gene Redlin as a conduit of his grace to me. He became president of CCC after the two former CEOs couldn't move the company forward just as technology was changing dramatically. Gene knew the industry from working in a smaller price-quote transmission service. We were spending $1 million or more a year on telephone lines to transfer data from every commodity exchange in the world to our Lombard office, then out to our customers around the nation.

At the receiver end we had proprietary software that helped people customize the presentation of prices, news, charts and analytics. We were just a year or so ahead of Bloomberg and others who were able to do this.

Comments from our professional clients reflected the value they got from our services. Jay Levine, veteran broker at Smith Barney said, "With a quick glance I can see where all of the major currencies are trading, real-time, twenty-four hours a day, and who is contributing . . . it's in edge." And Margie Cekander, commodity analysis manager at Keebler Company, wrote: "*Futures World News* beats their competition hands down when it comes to coverage of policy issues and USDA programs that affect markets."

Gene found that transmitting via FM sideband in some cities could drastically cut down costs. Then as satellite transmission became available, he put us on satellites, further expanding our reach and cutting our costs. We had sales offices with full time employees in Chicago, Los Angeles and Miami. Gene opened offices in New York and paved the way for Piers Fallowfield Cooper to open our London office, which gave us penetration into all of Europe.

Rex Wilmore stepped in to be CEO for a few years. He took Piers Fallowfield Cooper, our European managing director, under his arm and trained him on the complexities of running an organization. Rex renamed the company FutureSource after our new product line by that name. He coached the development team to create our unique FutureSource proprietary software that turned the company into a profit maker when our agricultural services were licking their wounds from the mid-1980s economic bust. He was the right man for the right job at the right moment.

Rex and I had some interesting business encounters while trying to get FutureSource up and running profitably. One was with a customer from London who was buying data from our company but sending the check to the home of our CEO. I fired the CEO, and Rex and I went to London to meet this guy. He was reselling our data to his clients, so we knew we had some leverage on him. In the first 10 minutes, Rex caught my eye as we farm boys both sized him up as a scam artist. We shut him off immediately, asked for prepayment before we sold him any more data, and three months later, we were happy to shut him off permanently for failure to make his next prepayment.

On another occasion we suspected that our data was being stolen and resold in Asia. "Let's find out by shutting off our data unannounced," I proposed. "Then we can reinstate customers one at a time as they call in complaining." Rex and others were a bit cool to that approach, but we did it, caught a few thieves, asked them to pay and moved on.
Life tip #66: Trust but verify.

We hired Doug McIntyre to be CEO of FutureSource. He was at the helm to help put together a sale to Bridge Telecommunications. When his unique management style seemed to get in the way, we brought in our lead salesperson, Chris Mahlmen, as CEO to lead us to the finish line. His skills and those of John Schillaci as CFO and general operations manager brought our organization to maturity. Each of these leaders brought unique and different skills that were needed at that particular time.

Chris's understanding of our marketplace, of the sales process and the complex world of software development led us to use the internet to greatly expand our horizons, cut our costs, and make us a candidate for acquisition. When we sold FutureSource in 2005, I breathed a great sigh of relief. **Life tip #67: Hire the right person at the right time.**

One unexpected repercussion of buying Commodity Communications Corporation was that the company we were using for global information, Commodity News Service, canceled our contract because they thought we would be in competition with them. When I got the word, I was walking down the hall with Rex Wilmore. He told me years later that I never broke stride but just said, "Well, then, we'll start our own news service."

And so we did. It was not a carefully planned decision, more a stroke of temporary arrogance out of necessity. We started *Futures World News* with Mike Walsten at the helm. It grew quickly but lost money for many years.

FutureSource got the attention of Rick Snape, who worked for Bridge Telecommunications in London. Rick's observation of our competitive edge with FM and satellite delivery whetted his appetite to acquire FutureSource. This led to Bridge acquiring a 40 percent interest in FutureSource. As part of that transaction, they provided news for our companies through their acquisition of Commodity News Service in Kansas City, so we shut down *Futures World News*. In late April 2001, I was visiting our London office when I got the word that Bridge had filed for bankruptcy. Who would acquire the 40 percent that Bridge owned in FutureSource? What would happen to Commodity News Service, our news source?

Within hours I called Terry Wooten and invited him to join me in building a new Futures World News organization. We would need to hire at least 30 journalists in Chicago, New York, Washington and London, as well as line up stringer correspondents from other far corners of the world like Africa's Gold Coast. Terry flew into action. We decided to get together in a few weeks to discuss his salary. As a former business associate, our mutual trust was so deep, money was a detail. Getting a news organization up and running quickly was the challenge. We were told we would lose our news by July.

I returned to our Iowa farm home to pray and ponder. I finally picked up the phone and talked with one of the reporters in Kansas City working for Commodity News Service. They had about 15 reporters, statisticians and weather analysts. I slipped down to Kansas City to hold a Sunday afternoon meeting with as many of their staff as wanted to show up for pizza. They all showed up. I told them of my plight. I knew theirs. They were about to be out in the cold. I made them an offer to stay on at their existing salaries, and we would launch a new global news organization. I lined up rental space, laid out our technical problems to Rex, and he sent the technical people to Kansas City to set up the data lines that were required.

In July of 2001, Paul Ingracia of the *Wall Street Journal* called me offering to provide news for us. He knew we were scrambling to rebuild a news organization because I hired a couple of his best reporters. He asked for a meeting in Chicago to lay out his hopes that he could satisfy our news needs. It was a tough meeting. I came into it under lots of pressure, running full speed with Terry and our technical staff to get our reporters around the world connected and working. I was frustrated with the unknowns that were hanging out there as a result of the Bridge bankruptcy.

Paul and his associates proposed that the *Wall Street Journal* take over our news needs by letting us resell their news to our customers instead of having our own commodity news source. Instead, I proposed that he sell us just the stories we wanted for $10,000 a month. He said no to that. He again pushed me to buy his entire data feed, which led to one of my most discourteous displays of arrogance and frustration of my career. "I don't want Dow Jones Commodity News! I know my customers' needs, and you guys are not good enough to service them. Period."

Paul, a mature, patient man, waited me out. Six months later our news service was up and running. I had hired several of his best reporters who had a nose for ferreting out news with price-changing potential. Paul knew we were serious competition. "How can we work together, Merrill?" he asked.

With that opening, I laid out what would work for our organization. "I will put my resources together with yours to form a new company. I get to pick which of your people are good enough to fit in. You find someplace else for the rest of them. We will share the costs and revenue sixty-forty."

"I think we can work something along those lines," Paul responded. "If you are a little open-minded on hiring some of our staff. What would you suggest we call the company?"

"Oster Dow Jones Commodity News," I replied.

We shook hands. We lost money for the next two years. The joke was on me. I got hit with 60 percent of the loss. But when we sold FutureSource and I no longer needed news, I exercised my option in a buy-sell agreement that Steve James had negotiated. Dow Jones wrote me a seven-figure check and immediately dropped the Oster from the Oster Dow Jones Commodity News company name.

At the outset it was a potential mess in the making, but by August it was up and running, with many glitches. The industry did not seem to notice our glitches, downtime, dropped stories and missing timely reports because another bankruptcy was making global news. Enron declared bankruptcy and took several of our customers down with them.

To add to the chaos, one of our London reporters had picked up a rumor that Enron was going bankrupt a week earlier. She had not fact-checked with anyone and went with the huge story with no other verification. I put her on leave for a week, giving me time to get to London to hear her story and decide with Terry if we should fire her. We had a productive educational meeting with her and kept her on. She was repentant, humble and open to our strong suggestions on how to operate in the future. That was September 10, 2001.

I was in our London office on September 11, 2001, when called to the small lunchroom TV as a plane crashed into one of the Twin Towers. Then the unimaginable—a second plane hit the second tower. A third plane hit the Pentagon. We learned days later that a fourth plane, probably aimed at the White House, was forced to crash in Pennsylvania by passengers led by a Wheaton college graduate, Todd Beamer, whose famous words "Let's roll!" still stir up strong emotions.

Numb from watching the Twin Towers implode and emotionally drained by listening to second-hand reports from our frightened New York FutureSource staff, Piers Fallowfield Cooper, our managing director, and I grabbed an early London dinner, fumbling for words to try to explain the actions of the day. Piers was experienced in terrorism through the difficult Irish conflicts and helped me think through what to do the next day.

A few weeks earlier one of our associates, Ari Jacobs, had what he called the toughest conversation of his life, telling me he was leaving our company for an even better financial opportunity with Waters, a financial information company. Waters held a conference on September 11 at Windows of the World, a restaurant at the top of the first tower. We knew Ari was probably at the meeting but held out hope that he somehow might have either missed the meeting or found his way down the smoke-filled stairs. Our hopes were not realized.

As the sun set over London, we knew neither the whereabouts of Ari nor our FutureSource office staff who ran in panic when the dust from the second tower blinded everyone within six blocks. Our office was only three blocks from the Towers. It would be Monday before all of our staff could be found. Ari was never found.

On Sunday morning the thought of an impending Third World War crossed my mind. I was staying at the London Hilton on Park Lane surrounded by Arabs who were in a very different mood than we Americans who were trapped in the hotel. I headed for Nicki Gumbel's church in Brompton, looking for Christian friends. The first thing the pastor did after the opening hymn was to ask every American to come forward so the Brits could pray over us. I felt the firm touch of a man's hand on my shoulder as they prayed for us. It was as if the Lord himself had touched me. I wept, breathed a sigh of release and felt like I was no longer alone in London. In times of crisis, it sure is good to be around praying friends.

Several days after the World Trade Center attack, United Airlines returned me to Chicago where I began to regroup with family and FutureSource staff and friends in Lombard. Our New York staff was in shock. After a day in Cedar Falls with Carol, I flew to New York where professionals were already helping our staff deal with the grief. Ari was a good friend. There was no trace of him. I talked with staff, recalled great memories of having been on the golf course with him only a few weeks earlier. We shed tears as we viewed the still smoking remains of the Towers.

Rick Snape was on my mind that week. In the past we had many interesting conversations about God, eternity and issues of the Christian faith. I called to see if he had time for coffee or a meal.

"Let's spend an evening together," he suggested. "I'll meet you at the Manhattan Ocean Club."

He shared his traumatic story of 9/11. As he had stepped off the commuter boat he looked up, saw people jumping from the towers, hurried back onto the boat and returned home, where he remained frozen in front of the TV between calls searching for friends.

"Is this a good time to reopen our conversation on spiritual matters?" I asked.

"Oh yes, Merrill. I need all the help I can get."

I gave him a new Bible and took him step by step through Dr. Bright's Four Spiritual Laws. He was not quite ready to ask God to come into his life, but he said he was surely going to consider the idea.

My radio-trained voice must have been projecting pretty well because a couple sitting at a nearby table came over and asked, "Can we buy you a drink? We heard a little of your conversation and would like to hear a repeat about the God stuff."

I was granted the privilege of going through the basics of the faith a second time with Rick in the presence of these London strangers who were in New York on business. I had never before been paid with wine to tell people about our Savior.

In the aftermath of all the 2001 tension, the Arizona Diamondbacks met the New York Yankees in the delayed World Series that finally got to game seven in early November. One of our Pinnacle Forum donors gave the organization third-base box seats to sell as a fundraiser. I offered $6,000, won the bid, and took my friend Dave Cavan. He had invested so much bringing prospects for Pinnacle Forum out to Iowa to hunt on our farms. It was the least I could do.

We got to see Louis Gonzales hit a bloop single just out of reach of the Yankee short stop in the bottom of the ninth to drive in the winning run for the Diamondbacks. Finally, the dark curtain of 2001 had lifted.

• • •

Carol and I frequently combined our international business travel, YPO travel and Campus Crusade trips. A stop in our London office in 1988 preceded the Berlin YPO University where we got a bus trip into East Berlin. We got up close and personal with Communist guards at the Brandenburg Gate and traveled nervously through Checkpoint Charlie headed to visit Bud and Shirley Hinckson. The Hincksons served with Campus Crusade in Eastern Europe and Russia. Bud worked with the Polish wrestling team and got them into Russia in 1988. He wrote me a letter asking for help.

Back at home in Iowa, I received the 1989 Iowa Entrepreneur of the Year award sponsored by Inc magazine and Ernst and Young. Oster Communications was awarded the Blue Chip Enterprise Initiative by the US Chamber of Commerce in 1992. We were recognized as one of the premier publishing and information organizations disseminating futures and options data.

I may have been the initiator on many endeavors, but our success came from the caliber of people and the uniquely different contributions of a highly talented team. I have mentioned some of these elsewhere, but let me repeat a little and add a bit of color.

Jerry Carlson developed economic information sources outside of traditional outlook specialists. He frequently gained big insight from his unusual sources. Rex Wilmore could edit *Pro Farmer*, write the best direct mail package, manage our internal staff and keep us on the cutting edge on computer information and delivery technology. He had a brainy guy named Mike Rodby who created the software we needed. I'm mentioning these names to underscore the uniquely different talents we possessed as team members.

Lee Searle had a unique way to play one economist off another to glean insights that only Pro Farmers received. Mike Walsten could extrapolate future price trends from piles of data farmers had no time to read. Larry Graham was a master at conducting our Professional Farmers of America seminars and making members feel like friends. Paul Wilcox and Glen Ring delivered unique analyses based on technical price action. Jim Weismeyer uncovered exclusives on his Washington beat that forced Secretaries of Agriculture to read *Pro Farmer* just to know what was going on in their own department. Kathleen Tanzy was quite a sight covering the White House for Future World News, especially when her five-foot stature was seen next to six-foot-seven Paul Volcker, one of her frequent contacts.

Dan Manternach was one of our best stage performers. Larry and Dan and others created a unique learning atmosphere that kept members coming back for more. Darrell Jobman made the pivot from agriculture to the world of futures when we acquired Commodities. Milo

Hamilton, a bit of an academic, took on the role of editor of Commodities Report. Jerry Becker's unique personal sales skills took our meager advertising program at *Commodities* magazine and grew it into a multimillion-dollar business.

David Yeager grew from a student part timer to lead our financial office as CFO. His steady hand over our finances is felt even today as a consultant to our family. Terry Wooten had an amazing grasp on how to find market-moving news. He came along to help Mike Walsten as we launched *Futures World News* and jumped back in to restart what would become Oster Dow Jones Commodity News when Bridge went bankrupt and left us without a news source. Len Swiatley came with our acquisition of American Graphics Services and grew it to a million-dollar business. Everything we produced went through Pete Cornell's highly talented art department.

Rex recruited Merlyn Vandekrol to do the heavy operational lifting in Cedar Falls when he took on the role of president of FutureSource in Lombard, Illinois. Merlyn was a trusted friend, advisor and general operations manager until cancer took his life as were completing the final sales of our companies. Tom Noon, with one hand on our financial books and the other on the Good Book, led us through turbulent times. He recruited Mike Klansek who was a huge asset in managing our money and handling the complexity of our FutureSource UK office in London.

Jim Wychoff was a quality writer who cranked out good stories for *Futures World News,* and his flexibility made him an anchor right to the end of our company run as we launched TraderSource. John Heidersbach, an award-winning wildlife artist, had a range of talent that included designing ads for our magazines and even writing the occasional direct mail piece. Chip Flory came to us with experience as a floor reporter on the Chicago Board of Trade. His contacts made him a great reporter and eventually the editor of the *Pro Farmer* newsletter.

Karen Gleason was an outstanding *Futures* magazine advertising salesperson. She mentored our daughter, Leah, when she joined *Futures* right out of college. Karen was involved in the futures industry, so her ability to open doors, even in London, was a vital part of our high-growth years for the magazine.

Life tip #68: Hire and cultivate unique skills.

Over the course of my business career, we started, acquired or revisioned more than 20 companies or divisions, including Communication Consultants, Professional Farmers of America, FutureSource, FutureSource UK, *Futures* magazine, Future World News, Oster Dow Jones Commodity News, Commodity Price Charts, Commodity Education Institute, Investor Publications, Corporate Risk Management, American Graphic Services, Pinnacle Prairie Real Estate, Oster Farms, *PorkPro*, Oster Partners, Commodities Hedgers and Traders, *Naperville* magazine, Parkade Properties, Cedar Falls *HomeTowner/Citizen*, Trader Source and Capitalist Edge. All told, we launched about 40 different products and services that impacted the business decision-making of 275,000 customers in the US and around the world. By the year 2000, we had small offices in 16 countries.

Some of the key launches over our first 20 years included the following:

October 1969: Started ComCo
December 1972: First Pro Farmer direct mail package dropped
March 1973: First Pro Farmer seminars in Peoria and Des Moines

March 1973: First issue of *Pro Farmer* newsletter
March 1974: First issue of *CornPro*
February 1976: Completed deal to buy *Commodities* magazine
February 1976: First issue of *PorkPro*
1977: *Management Monthly* launched
January '77: First issue of *Commodity Price* Charts
1978: *Commodities Closeup* newsletter launched
March 1979: First issue of *Landowner*
October 1980: Elanco signs deal with Oster to develop AgVision and Instant Update, the first electronic information service for farmers
March 1981: First day for AgVision and Instant Update
May 1981: Oster acquires Commodity Communications Corporation
December 1981: First day for Commodity World News, later renamed *Futures World News*, and later Oster Dow Jones Commodity News
December 1984: First issue of *Cedar Falls Citizen/ HomeTowner* serving 40,000 homes
Fall 1986: Version one of FutureSource
1988: Globalink offered to farmers
1989: Futurelink launched
January '89: First issue of *Futures International* edition
March '89: FutureSource opens London office
September '89: First issue of *Corporate Risk Management*
October '92: *Chart Insight* launched
August 2001: Launched Oster Dow Jones Commodity News

In 1992 the *Chicago Tribune* gave this birds-eye view of our companies in an article by William B. Crawford Jr.:

Oster Enterprises' Chief a Quiet Force
Behind Growth of Futures

It could be said that no private company reaches as many futures market members in as many different ways as does Oster's properties. Consider the breadth of his various enterprises which, together, operate in 16 countries, many through joint ventures with overseas partners.

Every day, 45,000 investors and hedgers at trading desks worldwide monitor real-time news, commodity prices, charts and technical analysis from Oster-owned publications and electronic data transmission services such as FutureSource, Futures World News and Pro Farmer Today.

Each week, 68,000 subscribers, primarily farmers and hedgers, receive a variety of Oster newsletters titled Land Owner, Trends in Futures and Commodity Price Charts.

Each month, 162,000 traders, brokers and institutional money managers look to *Futures* magazine, Oster's corporate centerpiece, for trends, analysis and other underlying fundamentals of the world's interlocking futures markets.

• • •

The trajectory of our companies was generally upward, but the ride was far from smooth. At one point in my career, I almost lost everything. In the mid-1980s, I had all the publishing companies cross-collateralized with farmland when Northern Trust called my loan. They sent a "hit man" to Cedar Falls to scare me by asking for the titles to my cars. He was quite successful.

I came home that night and told Carol it was possible that everything we have built could be down the drain. The company could be owned by the bank; we could be out in the cold with nothing. She said, "Oh, so what? We started with nothing. If we are supposed to have more, God will give it to us. If not, we're happy as a family." That kind of faith was a piece of our upbringing that I had lost sight of for a while. She brought me back to my grounding. Carol has always been a quiet but reliable conduit of God's grace to me.

My head dropped onto her shoulder as I wept a sigh of relief. Her impact on me and the future of our companies occupy only a few lines in this book, but that moment was one in which Carol became a conduit of God's grace, big time.

Darrell Jobman summarized the crisis situation this way:

> The company went through its biggest crisis during the agricultural depression of the middle 1980s. When the bank called Merrill's loan, precipitating a cash emergency, he called his executives to his home for a time of prayer and planning—a practice that continued for several months. Then he went to his department heads and confessed, "I've put this company in jeopardy because I've been too aggressive financially. I put my foot on the pedal too long. We're up on the high side of the track; we could crash if we don't take some immediate action."
>
> This candor helped build a closeness that is still part of the culture at Oster Communications. It also extended to those outside the company. "I went to our major suppliers and told them we couldn't pay our bills as timely as we had in the past," Merrill continues. "I asked for their patience and help. Out of a dozen suppliers only one said no. With their understanding and a bridge loan, we were able to pull through."

Life tip #69: Admit mistakes, ask forgiveness.

In the midst of the struggles, I recorded a prayer on September 4, 1985, that captures my desire to depend on the

Lord while using every business strategy I could think of to weather the storm.

> This morning the Psalmist reminds me, "Come and save me from these men of the world whose only concern is earthly gain—these men whom you have filled with your treasures so that their children and grandchildren are rich and prosperous. But as for me, my contentment is not in wealth but in seeing you and knowing all is well between us. And when I wake in heaven, I will be fully satisfied, for I will see you face-to-face" (Psalm 17:13–15 TLB).
>
> Yes, Lord, I can echo the words of the Psalmist. Thrust in the middle of a money-worshiping world, I struggle daily to maintain a sense of balance between pursuing excellence in business and having my eyes on earthly goals and longing after you, Lord . . . seeking to accomplish your will in my life. Even though these goals are not mutually exclusive, there are times when it would appear that spending too much time on earthly matters distracts one's focus on eternity. On the other hand, focusing on the mystical spiritual goals can equally cloud the way toward daily results in business, which provide witnessing opportunities.
>
> Lord, help me to find in each thing I do today an act of stewarding resources you have placed in my hands. Help me to make decisions regarding the future of our businesses which will be prudent, which will lay a base for the future so these opportunities to make this business a witness for Christ may be preserved until you return, if that be your will.

We moved into a real crisis mode for the first time in our lives. We tried to communicate openly and honestly to those who needed to know but otherwise kept it as quiet as possible to avoid compounding the damage. If you can't meet payroll, you sell something. So I began selling everything I had. Everything. There wasn't a thing I owned that wasn't for sale, either publicly or privately. I realized that I had been allowing myself to get too confident in my personal skills, and I admitted to the guys around me, "I've gotten us into a mess. If we're going to get out of it, it's going to take all of us." So we sat around the table at my house through a series of meetings in which we prayed and thought together and divided up responsibilities. God guided my business associates to take some bold actions.

Life tip #70: Prayer and fellowship lighten burdens.

During those very trying times, I sought help from my network of business and spiritual leaders. I had met Ron Blue at some History's Handful events, and I remembered a comment of his about money, "You can't take it with you, but you can send it on ahead, investing in kingdom-building properties." That mindset had a huge impact on the way Carol and I looked at our finances.

I reached out to Ron on a Thursday. After I explained my situation, he said, "Merrill, I could be there to help you tomorrow, but if you can wait until Monday, I'll bring a banker friend with me and we'll talk this through with you." I hung up the phone, broke down and wept because here was a man extending a conduit of grace to me just by showing he would drop everything to focus on my problems with no assurance of anything in return. That's grace.

Ron lined up a $2.2 million loan for me through a few Christians we both knew. I had to pay 25 percent on the money. Yes, you heard that, 25 percent. But the prime rate was 15 percent! That loan got me through until I was able to refinance the loan at a better rate with the help and recommendation by a longtime friend, Wendall Lockard. I was surrounded by people who were encouraging me when I wondered how I would make it from month to month. In one of my deepest pits, friend Gary Ginter, seeing the fear in my eyes, prayed, "Lord, take this fear away from my friend Merrill." He was at the right place at the right time with just the words God wanted me to hear.

The financial crisis forced me to seek spiritual guidance like that from Gary. I began devoting more time to prayer. I learned to fast, and I spent hours jogging rural Iowa roads in solitude as I talked with the Lord and listened to the Holy Spirit for guidance. I sought the advice of Ron Blue and other Christian peers and the senior executives at Oster Communications like our CFO Tom Noon and Chris Crane. With their counsel and the gentle nudging of the Holy Spirit, we turned the company around.

Despite the fact that our backs were to the wall, we didn't lose our entrepreneurial zip. We sized things up and decided we couldn't afford not to keep moving ahead in a fast-changing world. Contrary to what the bankers were insisting we do, we decided to drain cash from every area of the company to support FutureSource. Pour money into a hot idea. We invested about a million dollars in a technology change and software development over the next 24 months. It was a good decision but a high-risk one.

Some financial people were advising me to shut things down and lay off people. That didn't square with me, so we put all of our investable eggs in one basket and made a big bet right at the bottom of the market. The money we put into FutureSource allowed us to leapfrog the competition with new technology. It took 18 months for everyone else to catch up with us.

Years later I would repeat the practice of fervent prayer learned from the 1980s crisis. While doing a day in the desert with a friend, I was praying the Prayer of Jabez found in 1 Chronicles 4:10: "Jabez cried out to the God of Israel, 'Oh, that you would bless me and enlarge my territory! Let your hand be with me, and keep me from harm . . .'" The Holy Spirit convicted me that my borders needed no further expansion. Just the opposite. This was a game changer. **Life tip #71: Listen to the voice of the marketplace.**

I had begun to feel the Lord leading me out of the publishing business. Sometimes when you're led out of something, it's with a whack on the side of your head. For no reason at all, in my opinion, we got whacked in the head with a $900,000 fine because one of our customers supposedly lost a lot of money as a result of using our software. Well, the whole world was using our software, but this particular customer convinced the Commodity Futures Trading Commission that we were culpable. Despite feeling totally innocent, we wrote a check for $900,000 because our lawyer said it would cost us $1 million to defend against a $900,000 fine.

I didn't agree with the fine, but it was one of the signals the Lord used to convince me I didn't need to run businesses all my life. Businesses have unknown risks. I could enjoy another life. But it took us about 15 years to unravel the very complex set of companies we had put together.

A key person in all this was Steve James. Chris Crane brought him to my Scottsdale house to recruit me for Chris's board. As we served together on that board, I developed a great appreciation for Steve's business skills. When I got the vision of pivoting out of business into other ministry activities, I hired him to help me sell my companies.

When it came time to sell my companies, buyers paid big for access to recurring revenue streams like subscription and advertising revenue from *Futures* magazine, membership fees from Professional Farmers of America and monthly subscriptions to real-time data feeds from FutureSource. Collectively our companies generated $50,000,000 in annual revenue, mostly in recurring revenue.

We wound up selling Oster Dow Jones Commodity News to Dow Jones. We were able to sell American Graphics Services, which provided prepress service for Oster publications and other clients in the Midwest, to a man in Cedar Rapids for a very handsome figure just months before he and the whole industry went belly-up. We sold Professional farmers of America to *Farm Journal*. One by one we found buyers for each business, and by 2005 I had sold everything except my farming operation. I kept that for two or three more years. I made another pivot there from owning land for agricultural purposes to focusing on owning agricultural land in the path of development.

• • •

Why this shift from acquisition and expansion to downsizing and divestiture? A serious shift was occurring in my personal life. The late Bob Buford was a member of our advisory board. We had become friends through Young Presidents' Organization and its Christian subset, the Fellowship Focus Forum. In one of our board meetings he asked me, "Merrill, do you really want to be doing the same thing the second half of your life that you did in the first half?" By that time I had already been experiencing a parallel career through various projects with Campus Crusade for Christ.

I was motivated by the leadership of Dr. Bill Bright to begin thinking about using the experiences the Lord had given me in business to launch another career in Christian service even though in my mind I saw my businesses as a ministry but one that carried many unknown risks. I realized there's another world I could impact for eternity, the world of my business peers. It was this line of thinking that led to launching Pinnacle Forum America in 1996.

Over the course of my life, God has orchestrated a series of ideas, events, contacts and successes that represent a directional flow. Most new thrusts, passions, companies and ministries I have led have been a blend of the old, the new and the risky unknown. I wish I could tell Mom and Dad thanks for giving me the confidence to act on my beliefs to the point that I've been able to have a positive influence on others. That's the power of God flowing through conduits of his grace.

Life tip #72: The second half need not be a repeat.

Seven

Cedar Falls
Serving My Hometown

Oster Communications not only provides jobs,
but Merrill and his staff have contributed a great deal
to making Cedar Falls a great place to call home.
— Lee Miller, President, Cedar Falls Chamber of Commerce

A dear friend and mentor, Wendell Lockard, said to me the Sunday before Carol and I moved back to Cedar Falls, "When you get back here, Merrill, let's roll up our sleeves and do something for the Lord in this community." That gave me a sense of "You're welcome here. There's work for you to do." It was one of those one-liners that was a paradigm shifter and caused me to feel at home again.

The church was Downing Avenue Gospel Chapel in nearby Waterloo. I became Sunday School superintendent, song leader and elder. At one point I was spending about 20 hours a week doing various visitations and activities with Bob Smith Sr., a fellow elder. I trained the first group of deacons at Downing Avenue and would eventually donate Pinnacle Prairie land so it could become Bethany Bible Chapel in a highly visible location that helped stimulate significant church growth.

My relationship with Wendell continued over the years. In August of '82 we brought Dr. Bill Bright to Cedar Falls and Waterloo for a community-wide outreach. He spoke to a few hundred business people at our Sunnyside Country Club on how Christians can impact their culture. He also shared the gospel at our Rotary Club and in a Sunday morning service at Sunnyside, the fast-growing church in our community at the time. We used our business connections to advance the cause of Christ in our hometown.

Carol and I had an opportunity to get involved with Christian schools where our children attended. I became chair of the board for Christian Heritage, a small school with 50 or 60 kids in Cedar Falls. We were its major funders for several years until we folded it into the Walnut Ridge Baptist Academy in Waterloo. We have helped them raise funds for what is now Waterloo Christian School.

The Lord also provided service opportunities at Emmaus Bible College. Carol and I had studied their Bible correspondence courses and had greatly benefited from them. As vice chair of the board of trustees, I led the site selection committee to find a new home for the school in the early '80s. I had an airplane at the time, so I flew Dave Allison, Dave Glock and Dan Smith around looking at properties. We found one, and I helped work with the broker in Chicago to get the deal done. We relocated 200 students and 70 faculty and staff from Oak Park, Illinois, to Dubuque, Iowa. Later I was called on to chair the Vision '84 Capital Campaign, which retired the debt on the facility.

When we moved to Cedar Falls, my first office occupied 300 square feet on the Parkade. From that small start we grew into eight buildings along three Main Street blocks. Whenever a building next to one of our properties came up for sale, we bought it and moved in an Oster business. We were the dominant player on Main Street from a real estate standpoint. I started a real estate company, Parkade Properties, that did the buying and the renovating of the buildings. We improved a lot of properties and sparked the beginning of the turnaround of a very depleted downtown.

I wanted to give something back to the city that has given so much to me, so in 1990 I became the volunteer chair of the Chamber of Commerce. We commissioned a study group that produced a Vision 20/20 long-range plan for the future of Cedar Falls. I founded the Main Street Development Corporation with a group of six other businessmen-investors. We bought and refurbished properties to upgrade the downtown area. To help fund the program, I went door to door to get local businesses to sign up for a long-term taxing district.

The big idea was to create better retail spaces, fill the vacancies and attract higher quality tenants. We did it. We found good tenants like my friend Burton Field's Palace Clothiers. When we sold the buildings, we made a small profit. And then the ripple effect took over. Three other businessmen followed our example by renovating other buildings in hopes of making a profit. Within five years, 15 buildings had been renovated. The process of renewal continues today. Main Street is buzzing with restaurants, coffee shops and a host of new businesses.

Life tip #73: Leading by giving pays dividends.

Business owners have had a huge impact in our community over the years. I am upholding a tradition and an example set by my parents and hundreds who have volunteered time and donated money. We have a great community spirit. Over a 30-year period, there has been a dramatic change in the downtown Cedar Falls. I'm just one of many people who made this happen.

While chair of the Chamber of Commerce, I initiated a

Unity with Autonomy program with neighboring Waterloo Chamber Chair Donna Nelson. That initiative led to chambers joining after many years of bitter competition beginning when Waterloo leaders supposedly stole the county seat from Cedar Falls in the 1850s. When the local shopper, the *Cedar Bulletin,* went out of business, we started the *HomeTowner.* Then we added a weekly newspaper, the *Citizen,* that was inserted into the shopper. It later became part of the *Waterloo, Cedar Falls Courier.*

I was recruited by the Cedar Falls Community Theatre to co-chair the fund drive for the Restore the Regent Theatre campaign. The effort was successful, and the theatre reopened on September 10, 1994, under its new name, the Oster Regent Theatre. This was in honor of the $140,000 capstone gift Carol and I made in loving memory of my parents, Harland and Pearl Oster. The gift was made on the 25th anniversary of the founding of Oster Communications. **Life tip #74: There is joy in serving others.**

That same year, 1994, there was a strong push to bring casino-type gambling to our community. Many of my business friends were on the other side of this issue, but I took a public stand and used my influence and money to help defeat the measure. I was careful to let my employees and associates know that I was not pressuring anyone to support the antigambling campaign, but I felt the issue was important enough to address. I had a moral conviction against gambling, and I also felt that a gambling-based economy was not the type of economy to attract and keep quality businesses and people. I had a strong business incentive to keep the casinos out.

Several people encouraged me to get involved in politics, including some men from Grundy County who wanted to groom me as a candidate for governor. I told them I didn't feel called to go in that direction. I believed there were a thousand men or women in Iowa who would make good governors, but I was called to do something only I could do. I needed to fulfill my calling. This was an easy *no* because I felt so strongly that I was doing what the Lord wanted me to. And I knew that if I got too deeply involved in politics, it would suck up time, resources and energy.

I've had some brushes with national politics. I was a friend of Earl Butz, Secretary of Agriculture under President Reagan. We served together as members of the Central National Bank advisory board. Carol and I hosted US Congressman Cooper Evans and Secretary of Agriculture John Block at our home in Iowa for a fundraiser. One senator and World War II hero, Bob Dole, came to town wanting my help in raising money for his presidential run. That meeting set off a rumor I would be his secretary of agriculture. But it was only a rumor.

The local implications of national and international events were always on my mind as journalist and investor.

• • •

During this season of life, I had parallel careers going. I was running several businesses, increasing my farming acreage and operations, being active in community organizations, filling leadership roles in church and various Christian ministries. I didn't look at these different strands as different tracks. I saw them as one integrated whole where each area influenced the other.

At the center of it all was my family. They were an integral part of Oster Communications. Our children, David and Leah, attended company events with Carol and me. They became friends with our business associates and their children. Associates would come to the farm to ride horses and hunt pheasants. We were all learning how to grow a company, raise kids and be responsible community and church members.

Key executives shared our vacation home in Missouri, our boat and our "Green Machine," a 1976 GMC motor home. This sharing sometimes even applied to the company planes.

I bought an airplane primarily to get home faster after a speech. The airplanes we used to get to speeches and other events got larger over time. We had half interest in a Cessna four-seater with Irv Budlong. When a gust of wind trashed that plane while it was sitting on the ground at the Waterloo airport, I bought a Cessna 210 that had four seats facing each other, a jump seat in the back and, of course, the right seat next to the pilot. Then we bought a Cessna 421 with a pressurized cabin. Dale Hassman, Art Jacobs and Dexter Hyde were our pilots from 1976 to 1986.

There was another guy whose name I conveniently forget. He flew our plane to our summer home in the Ozarks just once. I found a bottle of whiskey in the magazine rack behind the right seat but never said a word. He got us back home, at which time I told him I would no longer be needing his services. This guy was mad at me. Oh man, was he mad. He stormed into my office, told me off and left without killing me. I never saw him again.

When members of our business family got in trouble, we all rolled up our sleeves and helped out. Ron Michaelson was the editor of *Pro Farmer* for a time and went on to handle several other important jobs at Oster. One night he got hit by a car while herding cattle that had strayed from his farm. I was the first one to the hospital to comfort his wife, Marcia, who still had blood on her clothes from holding Ron's head. We kept Ron on full salary for months while he recovered.

Another time Budd Moyer, who ran the *HomeTowner*,

had a fire at his house at two o'clock in the morning. By noon the next day, Oster employees had refitted the family with supplies and clothing from their own homes. This wasn't something I had to direct; it was just the fruit of our corporate culture.

That culture extended to other cities and countries as we expanded beyond Cedar Falls. By the end of the century, we had major businesses in Chicago, New York and London, with smaller offices in 16 countries. We were spread out, but we worked hard to stay connected. We celebrated our successes and comforted each other through our tragedies. The biggest was 9/11, discussed in the previous chapter. Our strong feeling that we were all part of a corporate family pulled us together in tough times.

Eight

Family First
Growing Together through Thick and Thin

You need another surgery, but it might kill you.
— Arizona neurosurgeon

Despite my civic involvement, business responsibilities and extensive travel, I rarely missed son David's soccer games or a game where daughter Leah was a cheerleader. Carol and I traveled the world, kids in tow: England, Germany, Japan, Australia, Mexico, Canada and more. Our airplane got me home quickly after speaking engagements. And I dragged David and Leah with me on many business trips. They picked up lots of education by skipping school and following Dad.

We always tried to get away for a week or two in the summer with David and Leah. One exception was in 1975 when we traveled all summer. I received the Outstanding Young Alumnus award in Ames that summer and headed straight for the Black Hills with Carol, David and Leah. Then across Wyoming and on to Vancouver via Lake Louise, down the west coast to California, home through Las Vegas and Denver. I was on the phone daily trading commodities, working with ComCo clients, discussing Pro Farmer initiatives, trying to keep businesses going while on a five week vacation.

David and Leah lived for the next Holiday Inn and a pool. I delivered one of my classic lines the kids won't let me forget. I was in the middle of a very tense contract negotiation with a Chicago client. He was yelling in one ear, the kids in the other. They were having fun, jumping on the bed but making it hard for me to hear my client, so I yelled to Carol, "Stick 'em in the pool." Not one of my better fathering moments, but unfortunately, one of the most memorable.

We got home from that trip to find that our Pro Farmer cruise down the Rhine had not met our guarantee, so we were going to pay for four people even though we had no customers. So the four of us jumped on a plane to Rotterdam, filled the unsold seats and finished the summer cruising the Rhine. There Carol took Dave and Leah on a side trip to see the home of Corrie Ten Boom while I was leading the farm group of a tour of soybean processing plants.

One time at the Chicago Open Board of Trade, a friend of mine, Bob Collins, saw my 10-year-old son picking up trading cards and asking questions. "Who is this midget you've got with you?" Bob asked. "He's asking adult questions." Years later, Bob sponsored David and helped him launch out on his own at the Chicago Mercantile Exchange as a market maker in the cattle options pit. David retired from the CME to be a real estate investor and broker.

We knew David was a man the day we were wrestling on the living room floor. He got lucky and somehow got his body under mine, stood up and carried me through the dining room. As he passed through the kitchen with me on his back, his mother screamed, "David, put your dad down. You might hurt him!" How humbling.

David got lucky again, trading a futures account in his mother's name. He was long silver futures as Bunker Hunt was trying to corner the market. His profits paid a good share of his Wheaton College education and set him on a futures-trading career path. He was called on in economics class to help teach futures to his classmates.

Both David and Leah had summer jobs in our company that motivated them to go to college. Leah, after a semester of data entry at our *HomeTowner* shopper offices announced, "I sure don't want to do that the rest of my life." Likewise, David, after a summer of scooping manure on the hog farm said, "I think I'd rather trade commodities like corn and beans than scoop hog manure the rest of my life."

We gave David and Leah a college graduation trip to any place in the world. But they had to take their parents along. It was one last chance to be one-on-one with them before they stepped out into the business world. David chose China, where we smuggled Bibles and almost got caught. We took Leah to Australia and New Zealand for her graduation trip in 1987. In typical fashion we threaded our multiple interests into one trip. We took in the YPO Hong Kong University, then on to Australia where I spent part of a day in our FutureSource Sydney office. That visit generated a 31-point memo faxed back to Rex Wilmore and Gene Redlin who were overseeing the company.

Initially I had thought about handing Oster Communications to David and Leah, but that's not the way things turned out. Long before I sold the companies, David had decided he did not want to be in publishing. He took a job in New York after college and then moved to Chicago and went to work for a friend of mine, Bob Collins of Green and Collins in the commodities industry.

Leah, on the other hand, did go to work for *Futures* magazine after college. She was the head of sales when

I sold the magazine. Shortly after we bought *Naperville* magazine, she became its publisher. When that magazine was sold, she continued to work for the new owner, the Chicago Tribune Company. Her immediate supervisor moved on to become senior vice president at Brookfield Zoo, and he later hired Leah. Today she is a vice president at Brookfield Zoo, overseeing a large staff responsible for sales, marketing and management.

● ● ●

It was on a family vacation to Hawaii in 1978 that I got the running bug. David and I were standing at the entrance of a sports store waiting for Leah and Carol to get out of the dress shop next door. A book title caught my eye and I bought *How to Run Your First Marathon*. That book changed my life. It had a daily schedule, starting with a 15-minute brisk walk on day one, which I did in front of the Westin Maui hotel. I followed the instructions, and by month nine I was ready for a 22-mile trial run in preparation for a full marathon two weeks later.

I entered the University of Northern Iowa (UNI) Marathon for my 22-mile run. I parked my car at the 22-mile marker. I had no intention of finishing. It was a cold, windy, late fall day with the wind coming from the west. Getting from Cedar Falls to Stout was real work against that wind. But with the wind at my back, I could tell at mile 21 that 22 would be easy. Then there it was—my Lincoln Mark IV. I kept on trucking, thinking that there would be friends at the finish line who would drive me back to get my car. But as I stepped over the finish line, the UNI track coach jumped out of his warm car, called out my time and introduced himself. I told him about my change of plans at mile 22, and he graciously drove me back to my car.

I ran 54 more marathons after that first cold, windy one, not to mention a few hundred 5K, 10K and half marathons. I found other guys in my neighborhood, members of the Cedar Rivers Runners Club, doing the same thing. Many of us ran together for 20 years. I ran Chicago several times, Drake, New York, London, Paris, Munich and others.

Now fast-forward a bit closer to life's finish line. Typically, I trained by running about 40 miles per week for 30 weeks for a marathon. That's 1,200 miles per marathon and 66,000 in preparation for 55 of them. Those miles took a toll on my body. In my late 60s after a long stretch of lower back pain and physical therapy treatments, my left foot quit working one evening.

It was the night of the *Naperville* magazine's Christmas party, 2009, hosted by Leah, our publisher. My back pain went into my leg, and I lost control of my foot. Foot drop is usually a precursor for back surgery, which took place two weeks later. Three days after surgery, a splitting headache signaled that I had a spinal fluid leak. A painful spinal tap followed, then a second surgery.

Two days after the second surgery, my headache returned, and I was diagnosed with spinal meningitis. Constant back pain, brain fog, dizziness and generally weak feeling set the tone for the next six months.

After a small recovery, we decided to retreat to Arizona for a few weeks. There we got a sobering second opinion from Barrows Neurological Clinic in Phoenix. The attending expert said I needed a third high-risk surgery to repair the first two. When I asked for a clear explanation of the risk, he responded, "Possible debilitation for life or death." We found his sales pitch a bit lacking and opted to look for other options. Next, we headed to Mayo Clinic where after two visits the neurosurgeon declared, "You will be in pain management the rest of your life."

Although the thought of impending death crossed my mind, Carol's constant upbeat presence and love kept me from falling into depression. But I was on the edge. My confidence in decision-making was deeply shaken. I looked to Carol as my lead partner, a new role for both of us. This normally soft-spoken woman insisted on getting more input when the surgeon signed off, in effect saying, "These things happen. I am sorry, but you need to find the best pain management specialist because yours will be a life of pain."

It was during those first nine months after surgery when the pain was most severe and the outlook was most bleak that I jotted down a list of thoughts and lessons the Lord was impressing on me:

1. Be still and know that I am God. Slowing the pace of life allowed me to see God more clearly. The book of James took on new meaning, especially James 1:2, "Consider it pure joy, my brothers and sisters, whenever you face trials of many kinds, . . ." James teaches that suffering is purposeful. God had my full attention while I was lying flat on my back, wondering if I would ever be pain-free.
2. God shows up in the face of people. Carol's constant care took on a new look; the hand and love of God at work as she tried to make me comfortable. When I saw the world through God's eyes, I saw Carol.
3. The more clearly I saw the Lord, the more disgusting I found my sin, and the more I appreciated 1 John 1:9. "If we confess our sins, he is faithful and just and will forgive us our sins and purify us from all unrighteousness." Lying on my back, looking to the heavens, I became more thankful as a forgiven sinner who has been saved by the blood of Christ.

4. I saw a bigger God and a smaller Merrill in my near-helpless condition.
5. I am not self-sufficient.
6. God is sovereign. He will take care of me. He knows the outcome.
7. If I can depend on the Lord for my eternal security, surely I should be able to depend on him for surgery recovery and temporal things like financial concerns.
8. I have learned to lean less on my own understanding.
9. I was freshly impressed how God hates sin, yet he makes me an heir to the throne.
10. Prosperity has made me depend less on God. I needed this setback to gain a new perspective. In this clearer view of life, I see my problems in light of God's power and in the context of a world where many people are suffering more than me.
11. I am not alone. Pinnacle Forum friends, church friends, neighbors and acquaintances around the world have been praying for me. That's humbling.

Life tip #75: Count your blessing in times of crisis.

I experienced what I had been teaching in Pinnacle Forum and other settings: trials mature us, humble us, help us compare our problems to the size of our God, not the size of ourselves. The lessons of the faith that have so easily rolled off my tongue were now moving from my head and settling deeply in my heart. Hopefully, the lessons would reshape my character so my actions could help make this a better world if God granted me more time.

He did. We have found new ways to mentor, new ministries to accelerate, new people to introduce to God's unfailing love. Through it all, the Lord gave me a clearer view of himself and my dear wife. It was through Carol's eyes that I saw a new and deeper dimension of love than I had ever experienced.

Carol is the unsung heroine of my life and the success of the Oster companies. In the early years of our marriage, our differences frustrated us. But later in life we found that our unique strengths and weaknesses complimented each other. During one of our little flaps when we thought we had irreconcilable differences, our family doctor, Bob Bremner, held up an open hand with fingers spread wide. He pointed to the tips of the fingers and the valleys in between as my strengths and weaknesses. Then he opened his other hand and pointed to the tips and valleys as Carol's strengths and weaknesses. Then he brought the two hands together and interlocked the fingers into a prayerful pose. "You see," he said, "God created you with unique strengths and weaknesses so that *together*, you will be stronger."

We have been to a dozen marriage seminars, have read 20 or more books and heard many sermons on the topic, but that one illustration in Bob's office clicked like no other counsel in both of our minds. Today we laugh at the way I see the big picture, yet repeatedly forget to lock the patio door. And we laugh at Carol's insistence on details like straightening and cleaning the house before the cleaning ladies arrive. We are truly opposites who are attracted to each other like magnets today.

When we were looking for a home in Scottsdale, the broker opened the door, and I walked straight through the house to the patio to check out the view overlooking the pool, golf course, a small lake with Camelback Mountain in the background. I whispered to Carol, "We are buying this house." She responded, "Did you even look at how chopped up the house is?" "Nope," I said. "You can change the house, but you can't change the view." We bought the view. And she beautifully took care of the details inside. I see the big picture; Carol sees what I overlook.

During my physically challenging times, seeing Carol's face was like seeing Jesus. She helped me develop a new overcomer outlook. Once again I saw a bigger Lord and a smaller Merrill. I began to think, "I am in God's hands—not sure what future he plans, but let's just take a day at a time and be thankful for those intermittent pain-free moments." I decided to continue looking for a doctor whose prognosis was more in keeping with my growing confidence that it would turn out just fine.

We found him. A neurosurgeon at Loyola looking at the lump on my back said, "I've seen a dozen or more of these spinal fluid leaks. Keep up with your therapy. Give it a year, it will dissolve." He was prescribing patience! That has been a rare quality in my life. I thought I had turned my life over to the Lord, but this time I learned to wait, yet to diligently do everything my therapists recommended while waiting. **Life tip #76: Get multiple second opinions.**

God was at work when I found a therapist who could push me through to full recovery. David Bokerman was about the age of my oldest grandchild. I found David after I had a full knee replacement, a further complication of my running life. He told me, "Your previous therapists have helped you get temporary relief by dealing with your symptoms. Let me give you a protocol that deals with your basic remaining problem."

David nailed it. My knee became more flexible, and my back pain disappeared. The stretching and strengthening exercises worked. Finally, after playing a round of golf, I felt no need for pain meds. My first surgery was in December 2009; my first pain-free month was July 2018. And by the grace of God, in 2019 I have had pain-free months and have returned to jogging, biking, golfing and hunting, each at a slightly—no, significantly—slower pace than before but with no pain! Whereas I had taken good health for granted, now I frequently pray. "Thank you, Lord, for another day of good health."

Life tip #77: Thank God daily for good health.

• • •

I have been quite active in organizations outside of our own companies. In addition to my involvement with local organizations in Iowa like the Cedar Falls Chamber of Commerce, Community Main Street, the YMCA, Western Home, Iowa State University, University of Northern Iowa and the Hawkeye Institute of Technology, I have belonged to many national organizations and ministries. I got exposed to CBMC (Christian Business Men's Committee) after college and attended some meetings.

Over the years I've had dealings with Fellowship of Companies for Christ International (FCCI), Walk Through the Bible, and other fine organizations. I became part of Young Presidents' Organization (YPO), an organization for business leaders who become presidents of $5 million companies or larger before reaching age 40. There's a Christian group within YPO, and I made some great connections there and participated in their forums.

But by far the group that had the most profound impact on me and with which I've had the most involvement was Campus Crusade for Christ. Out of my roots in Crusade there would grow the ministry I was put on this earth to help create—Pinnacle Forum.

Nine

Pinnacle Forum America
Changing the World Together

A few influential people led by God to do the right thing
at the right time can change the culture. You can make a difference.
You can change the world.
—Dr. Bill Bright, founder, Campus Crusade for Christ

Milo Hamilton, one of our reporters at *Futures* magazine and *Futures World News*, got an interview with Nelson "Bunker" Hunt in 1979 while he was trying to corner the world's silver market. *Futures* magazine was one of the few publications Bunker talked to during this time. As Milo was leaving, Mr. Hunt asked, "Who's your boss?"

"Merrill Oster," Milo told him.

"Give this to Merrill Oster."

It was an invitation to an executive weekend in Palm Springs sponsored by Here's Life, a Campus Crusade for Christ ministry.

We gladly accepted, and in February 1980 Carol and I joined 100 couples at a Here's Life weekend. We mingled with leaders and celebrities like Bunker Hunt, Bill Armstrong, Roy Rogers and Dale Evans. We were ministered to by Dr. Bill Bright, founder of Campus Crusade for Christ. He challenged us each to give or raise $1 million to become part of History's Handful, a small group who could make a big difference by financing Crusade's various national and international missions to change the world for Christ.

Carol and I later signed the pledge. We had gone to the weekend retreat to see Bunker Hunt. Dr. Bright was thrown in as a bonus! He would have a profound impact on our lives. From 1979 through the early 90s, I had the opportunity to serve with him on various committees. He invited me to be on the executive committee of History's Handful to help recruit other leaders. He also asked me to serve on the board for Here's Life publishing company and the Year of the Bible committee and numerous host committees for Here's Life weekend events.

Carol and I invested in several translations of the *Jesus* film into other languages. Our son David and I accompanied Dr. Bright to Japan for a staff conference and to Moscow for a pastors' conference. Carol and I were in Russia when Crusade launched the *Jesus* film in Moscow and St. Petersburg in a massive effort to evangelize those just being freed from the shackles of communism. The Berlin Wall had fallen, the Iron Curtain had opened and people were hungry for the gospel. They lined the streets wherever Westerners were passing out Christian literature.

We were in Moscow waiting for the theater to open for the debut of the *Jesus* film. I was sitting on the curb with Bunker Hunt. Bunker and his wife, Caroline, had invested $30 million to launch the *Jesus* film. "Bunker, I am a curious journalist," I said. "If I'm not being too intrusive in this ministry setting, can you tell me if it's true that you've been left with nothing in the aftermath of the silver trade debacle?"

"Oh yes, Merrill," he replied. "Nothing. Of course, in Texas you can keep your home and a few horses and personal things. If you added it all up, it wouldn't amount to more than three or four million dollars."

I had watched dozens of Iowa farmers go through bankruptcy. In Iowa, nothing is nothing.

"So, Bunker," I asked. "What is your take away from the silver trade?"

His response is a classic. "Never be long in a marketplace where the shorts can change the rules."

Bunker and his allies owned so much silver that markets were skyrocketing when the New York Mercantile board changed the rules. They halted trading, then let the shorts get a break by allowing no new longs in the market. Prices plummeted. Bunker lost billions. He was a believer in Christ, but his manipulation of the futures market left a pretty sour taste in my mouth. Nonetheless, he made some important contributions before the Lord took him home.

At one point Carol and I took a taxi ride to a neighboring town 10 miles outside Moscow. I watched as she handed an elderly lady a copy of *The Four Spiritual Laws*. Carol pointed to heaven, crossed her hands over her heart and then pointed to the lady, trying to communicate that God loved her. The lady was surprised that the little booklet was a gift and teared up as we drove away. We expect to see that dear soul in heaven.

Because of the initial success of the *Jesus* film in Russia, Dr. Bright returned on a few other occasions. David and I were with him on one trip during which he took us into a Kremlin building where we met with one of the top people in the government. As we walked out of that meeting he said, "There, Merrill. I've just shown you how to influence the most influential people in the world." It was a moment I'll never forget. He was basically saying, "Be bold enough to ask for an invitation. When you get there, be bold enough to share Jesus Christ with them."

And not just in the Kremlin. We watched him witness to a cab driver. From the time he picked us up until we got to our destination, Dr. Bright asked him about spiritual things. "I'm hearing about this all over the city," the driver said. "What is going on? I want to know more about Jesus." Dr. Bright led him to Christ before we got out of the cab.

It's that kind of mentoring that gave me the confidence and ability to encourage others to do the same. Carol and I have passed out a few thousand of Dr. Bright's *The Four Spiritual Laws* to our acquaintances and to strangers as we traveled around the world.

Life tip #78: Share your faith to change the world.

A few years later I returned to Moscow to see a week-long event sponsored by a consortium of ministries called Commission that was claiming amazing numbers were coming to Christ in a Russian revival. I invited an English speaking taxi driver to attend the meetings and help me interact with the locals. After the first night, the driver, Andre, said the talk about God was interesting and the name Jesus was totally foreign to him. He asked if I could get some of the free literature for his son. After the second night, he asked for literature for his wife. After the third night, he asked me to come to his home and explain all of this Christian information to his family.

We ate a wonderful home-cooked meal and chatted about Jesus. I helped introduce Andre's family to Jesus Christ. Each made a personal decision to follow Christ. I knew God was working in their hearts. As I was leaving, Andre's wife, Galena, said, "Thank you for coming to our home. There is a Chinese proverb that says, 'When there is a need, at just the right time, the provision will come.' You came to our home at the right time."

I visited Andre and Galena a few years later and found them growing in their faith.

Life tip #79: Some yearn for Christ. They need your help.

• • •

Over a 10-year period I was exposed to ideas about cultural change and the ministry of the Holy Spirit at several weekend retreats held by Dr. Bright. I met leaders like Ted Engstrom, who headed up of Youth for Christ and, later, World Vision, and Ron Blue, founder of National Christian Foundation and Kingdom Advisors. At a History's Handful retreat in January 1993, Dr. Bright brought a sobering and inspiring message:

> In spite of all the good efforts of our churches and Christian ministries, the cultural decay in America has accelerated over the past 50 years. The reason: There is a relatively small number of highly influential people, cultural gatekeepers whom we are not reaching with the message of Christ's transformational power. You businessmen have the credibility, influence and convening power to get the ears of these people. A small number of people have led America down this path of cultural decay, and a small number can turn America to positive biblical solutions to solve today's problems.

As a small group of us broke up, Dr. Bright turned to me and said, "Merrill, I would like you to pray about providing leadership to an effort to reach the cultural gatekeepers in every arena of American society." I was moved by his personal challenge and ready to accept. God had been preparing me through a series of business and personal growth experiences since my first History's Handful weekend a dozen years earlier.

Several months after I had joined the organization and pledged $1 million, the financial foundations of the agriculture and commodities industries began to collapse. Subscriptions plummeted for *Futures* magazine, *Futures World News* and Professional Farmers of America. Customers dropped the pricing-and-market analysis provided at FutureSource and Professional Farmers of America. Oster Farms reeled under a sharp drop in land values. And then the bank called my loan.

I related this economic crisis of the 1980s and how we survived it in Chapter 5. The ordeal eroded my self-confidence, but the Lord used it to teach me the vital role peer relationships could play in solving problems and providing spiritual support. By the end of 1986, our companies were back on their feet, and I was fellowshipping with believers across the country through History's Handful and the Fellowship Focus Forum, a small Christian group that was part of the Young Presidents' Organization (YPO). The development of peer relationships via conference calls and face-to-face meetings was something I valued highly and would later strive to recreate through Pinnacle Forum.

Life tip #80: Trials prepare us for the next assignment.

I felt a growing desire to challenge influential people, mostly fellow CEOs, by reminding them that our culture had gone to hell in handbasket in the last 50 years, and it had happened on our watch. I believe a few of us can turn things around by getting the cultural gatekeepers we know to think and act according to Christian principles. If we follow our passion to serve society in ways that move us beyond mere success to true significance, we can change the world.

In 1995, two weeks after Dr. Bright asked me to lead the ministry to reach the country's cultural gatekeepers, we talked again. The challenge he gave would allow me to blend my business and entrepreneurial skills with my experiences in YPO and other nonprofit organizations. The Lord had been preparing me mentally and spiritually for a change.
Life tip #81: A few influencers can change cultures.

Initially, Dr. Bright's staff had a plan for implementing this program, and he put me in touch with his consultant, Cindy Cutler. She had done some research and drawn up a set of recommendations. Dr. Bright also arranged a series of weekend brainstorming sessions with various Crusade supporters. These sessions provided invaluable ideas and connections with business leaders like Craig Lawrence, Norm Miller, Arch Bonnema and Ray and Mary Berryman. Other advisors included Allen Morris, Tom Weins, Sid Wright, Steve Douglas, Jim Corman, Grant McCabe and Bill Dodder.

I came to the conclusion, however, that the Crusade plan of large international gatherings of influential leaders didn't fit my background and experience. I returned the portfolio I'd been given and said, "Why don't you find somebody else to do this particular version of reaching the culture? I have some ideas of my own." I'd started and grown a few organizations from scratch. And for many years I'd been a part of Fellowship Focus Forum, a group closed to anyone outside of Young Presidents' Organization. Getting leaders together to encourage spiritual growth that leads to passion-finding and cultural impact seemed like the logical thing to do.

Bill Dodder, a Crusade staff member, had been working on the distribution of the *Jesus* film in the greater Phoenix area and had a heart for influencing the influencers. He recruited

Terry Hamlin to join us. On a hike up Pinnacle Peak in North Scottsdale in 1995, the three of us prayed over Phoenix and the surrounding cities. We asked the Lord for direction in starting a ministry to the most influential 1 percent in the region. We asked for signs that we were moving in the right direction.

We started Bible studies using a Forum format where we could establish relationships, and we used golf outings to meet key leaders and share our vision. Several months later a breakthrough occurred when we were asked to help organize the 1996 Super Bowl XXX breakfast sponsored by Athletes in Action with the assistance of Jerry Colangelo, general partner of the Phoenix Suns, and Mike Ingram of El Dorado Holdings. We followed up the breakfast by inviting the list of attendees to various events designed to build relationships that led to Forums.

In July 1996 we convened a retreat in Beaver Creek, Colorado, to officially launch Pinnacle Forum. Terry Hamlin was asked to be the executive director of the prototype Phoenix chapter. Our mission statement read that Pinnacle Forum existed "to encourage and equip influential leaders through confidential Forums, supported by a national network, to engage in personal and cultural transformation that honors Jesus Christ."

The foundation we were building upon went back to 1975 when Bill Bright and Loren Cunningham, founder of Youth With a Mission, met for lunch. God simultaneously gave each of them a message to give to the other: "The culture is shaped by seven mind-molders or mountains in society. If we can influence each of these areas for Christ, we will win the culture of our nation." The Seven Mountains of Culture they identified are: Arts & Entertainment, Business, Education, Family, Government & Military, Media and Religion. Our Pinnacle Forum initiative would hopefully surface leaders interested in impacting one or more of these mountains.

We needed some funding to get the program off the ground. I put up $100,000 and challenged Dave Cavin, Foster Friess and John Lang to each do the same. Mike Ingram and Roger Roberson joined shortly thereafter with very significant investments of time and money. We put together a series of pheasant hunts on my farm in Iowa to raise interest in Pinnacle Forum. I've always used my farms to further Christian causes. I remember a statement my grandmother made when I got my first car. "Everything you have, including this car, is the Lord's," she told me. "Use it for his purposes."

Being together for two or three days in the field deepens your relationship with one another as you walk and talk and encourage each another. One guy gets excited about something, and another guy will say, "Well, I'm not particularly excited about that, but here's my passion." These conversations are opportunities to see the Lord shine through other men's lives in a unique setting.

On one hunt Joe Foss came as a speaker, and he attracted some great people. He was a World War II Medal of Honor winner who went on to become governor of South Dakota, commissioner of the American Football League and president of the National Rifle Association. He had been volunteering his time with Dr. Bright, and that's how we met.

I had also bumped into another World War II hero living in Scottsdale and invited him to come on the pheasant hunt. His name was Kenny Dahlberg. We had two of the most decorated aces of World War II sitting around our dinner table debating who had the toughest Word War II stints. These guys were genuine heroes. They helped create an atmosphere for us to enjoy fellowship with some pretty high-powered people.

In 1997 we began a lecture series sponsored by Jerry Colangelo to reach a large number of leaders in the greater

Phoenix area. Attendees heard speakers including Dr. Ravi Zacharias and Os Guinness challenge them to make a connection between issues of faith and outcomes in America's culture. Bill Dodder, Terry Hamlin, Mike Ingram, Dave Hall and others made follow-up calls inviting leaders into intimate Forums where they could discuss current issues in the light of Scripture.

Some leaders who spent their winters in Phoenix and attended the lecture series carried the Pinnacle Forum idea to their hometowns. Roger Roberson was the first. He took the Forum concept back to Champaign, Illinois, and started several Forums with the help of Phil Reed as executive director and Rick Stevens and Steve Hillard as Forum facilitators. Both Rick and Steve were also solid financial supporters and godly leaders who helped us launch Pinnacle Forum nationally.

The Lord opened another venue to meet leaders who had an interest in spiritual development and cultural change. The founders of the Joe Foss Leadership Breakfast held on Good Friday were looking for help. Bill Dodder and I approached Bob Kane, who was responsible for the breakfast. Bob was the convention manager at the Boulders Resort and head of the men's ministry at Scottsdale Bible Church. We told him how the breakfast could be revised and used as a model for other cities if it were upgraded to a top-notch site with world-class speakers. He invited Pinnacle Forum to take over the event. Terry Hamlin, as he had done so many times, rose to the occasion and made the breakfast a success. Under his leadership it became a large-venue event with 700 to 1,000 attendees where Pinnacle Forum Partners could bring their peers.

In addition to these large events, we also used hunting, fishing and golfing trips to share the vision. Pinnacle Forum groups sprung up in various parts of the Phoenix valley. Terry's wife, Becky, started the first Forums for women leaders. While the original goal was to be a national organization, for the first few years we focused exclusively on the Phoenix area. Two members of the local board made their support contingent on exclusive attention to Phoenix for two years before doing a national launch. While initially a limitation, working in a smaller region helped us lay a solid foundation for this new organization.

The first Forum was a prototype held in one of my friends offices. We meet for about a year to test the idea and so that 10 guys who had the experience could then talk about and duplicate it. Pinnacle Forum groups provide a confidential, invitation-only setting where peers coach each other with lessons learned from their own life stories, observations and struggles. Partners get and give information, sometimes from Scripture, sometimes from experience. The safe environment is a context where "iron sharpens iron" and where it's possible to hear the Spirit's quiet voice.

The Forum I attended in Scottsdale had a profound impact on me when I began to have some business troubles as a result of the economy going backward. I admitted to my Forum that every stock market and real estate decision I'd made in the last two years had been bad. They assured me that I wasn't alone. The stories of how others planned to cope with the situation provided some fresh insight and perspective. We prayed for each other. I received new energy and the feeling that my Partners were in this high-stress time with me. We all eventually survived the 2006 financial crisis, humbled and blessed.

Our group included Ralph Palmen, Roger Roberson, Russell Wolfe, Karsten Solheim and Mike Burns. Ralph, Roger and Mike each served as chairman or CEO of Pinnacle Forum. Here's just one example from this group of how Pinnacle Forum is designed to work. One day Ralph said,

"We talk about culture change. Russell has been actually doing stuff in a key area without talking too much about it. Let's go see him and find out more about Pure Flix."

Russell was cofounder of the film production company Pure Flix, which has produced and distributed nearly 100 faith and family-friendly movies. What he shared with us motivated a few Partners and friends to raise about $6 million to help Pure Flix roll out the movie, *God's Not Dead*. Russell produced and costarred in the movie, which grossed almost $65 million against a budget of $2 million. Pinnacle Forum Partners are credited with helping launch Pure Flix with their investment in *God's Not Dead* and other Christian films.
Life tip #82: We can accelerate someone else's passion.

As Pure Flix was building on this success with a second film, Russell was stricken with Lou Gehrig's disease and passed away in 2015 at age 50. He had a big influence on getting some of us involved in a project that has had an impact on Hollywood. The Christian market got exposed to Hollywood filmmakers through Pure Flix, which continues to put out quality Christian-themed films.

• • •

Pinnacle Forum's relationship with History's Handful and Campus Crusade provided an initial challenge. We sensed a conflict with some Crusade staff who saw Forum participants as prospects to be cultivated for donations. When we decided to move forward as an independent organization, Dr. Bright gave us his blessing. He generously offered contacts and resources and gave our young organization the freedom it needed, yet he made Campus Crusade staff available as counselors and encouragers whom we have utilized and valued.

During the early years, Dr. Bright called me probably once a month. He would ask, "Merrill, how are you doing?" One time I shared some of the tough experiences we were having. I told him we were nowhere near as large as I thought we would be at this stage. He said, "I've been at this all my life, and we've never been successful at consistently bringing together groups of highly influential people, the likes of which you are doing in Pinnacle Forum. The best is yet to come." He encouraged me to keep looking up and keep pressing on.

Pinnacle Forum America (PFA) was launched nationwide in 2001. I was the president and chair of the board. The other members were Rich Broggi, Steve Hoeft, Richard Macleod, Michael Regan and Roger Roberson. Our advisory board included many well-known Christian leaders such as George Barna, Ken Blanchard, Bob Buford, Chris Crane, James Kennedy, Bill McCartney, Alan Sears and Joseph Stowell.

I turned my positions over to Ken Willig in 2001 when business pressures required my attention. Ken, along with Ralph Palmen, Mike Burns and Dwight Olsen, had established a Chapter in Seattle and planted seeds in a dozen other cities. After Ken's tenure, we invited Ralph Palmen to become president. Ralph had exceptional leadership skills and put together a lot of the organizational structure that we needed to grow. Our current president and CEO is Guy Rodgers, former vice president of a polling company and founder of two political consulting and strategy firms and a godly leader. Bruce Everette, a retired executive vice president of retail operations for Safeway, provides leadership as board chair and has put excellent organizational structure in place. He has mentored me on how to bring out the best in a board.

PFA is effectively organized to bring eight to 12 Partners together into local Forums. In 2004 we created the Pinnacle

Forum Foundation, which provided matching funds to launch new Chapters. By 2018 PFA had impacted thousands of men and women as prospects and through almost 80 active Forums in nine Chapters around the nation.

In addition to Forums there are local events where Partners connect with other leaders in their area. We also offer Video TeleForums where Partners meet in confidence to discuss and apply the biblically based ideas on how to bring about personal and cultural transformation. We're seeing some of the same results in video forums as we do from those meeting face-to-face. Today, Chuck Bryant, a business friend from California, is seeing amazing growth in these video forums.

PFA hosts a National Conference focused on education, inspiration, challenge and motivation. We also started the Pinnacle Forum Institute for Leadership Transformation deigned to help Partners assess where they are as a cultural change agent and learn how to move to the next level. They learn how to leverage their existing leadership skills into powerful spiritual influence.

Our thrust today is exactly what it was when we started: to attract leaders and give them a confidential place to meet and talk about their spiritual and personal development as well as their cultural impact. In the process we help each other move beyond focusing on earthly success to finding eternal significance through pursuing our God-given passions. We haven't arrived; we're just arriving. There's so much to do, and we can't do it in our own strength as we have so often done in building our own businesses. We will do it as God leads and provides.

From the outset, Bill, Terry and I asked the Lord to show us some evidence that we were on the right track. It has come in the consistent flood of stories of life change as a result of being involved with Pinnacle Forum. Many, many times

I've heard statements like "I've been waiting for something like this all my life," or "This is exactly what I needed. I felt alone and isolated, but not anymore."

Kelvin Cochran is the former fire chief of Atlanta. He was fired in 2015 because he expressed his religious beliefs in a book. About six months ago he joined a video TeleForum. He is now on our national board. In our interview he said, "I didn't realize the need I had for a group of men around me who could support me like I do today. Within six weeks of being in Pinnacle Forum, I realized how badly I needed what I didn't even know was available."

A pastor once told me, "I don't know what you guys did to my friend, but he was just a pew sitter until he got involved in Pinnacle Forum. Now he's more active in our church as well as Pinnacle Forum." Pinnacle Forum does not compete with the church. We accelerate the impact of churches in our communities by helping people support or start ministries that are in line with their passions. At the same time, Partners need to step outside of their churches and work with each other irrespective of doctrinal differences. Institutional religion often gets in the way of creating a deep personal relationship with the living Lord.

Partners discuss big issues, pray together, come alongside when we need each other. Each person has his or her passion in some area where God is leading. Rick Warren says, "God gives us different passions so that everything he wants done in the world gets done."

So how does a Forum get started? Here's one example: My friend Ken Lockard invited his friend John Walker to our National Conference. John invited his college roommate Roger Berris to join them at the Scottsdale, Arizona event. When they introduced me to Roger, we found that we both belonged to Stonebridge Country Club in Aurora, Illinois. When we got back home, we invited Bill Read and my neighbor, John Calamos, to join us for golf. We decided to start a Forum by inviting a few guys we knew and had common interests. Over the next few months, Angelo Kleronomos, Chuck Podczerwinski, Mel Tradeau, Rich Grischeim and Mike Rushin joined us. Mike moved to Phoenix, and we added Bill Buschar, and most recently, Tony Pulgine heard about us on LinkedIn and joined.

We meet every other Saturday at the club boardroom, discuss our prayer requests, study a book, and frequently will get a tee time to follow the meeting. We get together with our wives at least twice a year in a restaurant or in one of our homes. The opportunity to have a group of peers talking about personal and cultural change has stimulated each of us to embrace an accelerated rate of spiritual growth and community involvement in culture-changing activities.

One of our guys got excited about an inner city mentoring program. The ministry is seeing significant changes in young men who are finding father figures in a mentor. Another man and his wife have started a Christian school. Another guy launched a program to help youngsters determine if they've got a heart defect, inspired by his son's death from a heart defect. And when one guy gets excited about something, it usually draws three or four of us in to help them out in some way.

One of our Partners called attention to the fact that right in our backyard, Aurora, Illinois, we have the third or fourth largest Planned Parenthood baby-killing factory in America. Because of his leadership and passion, our Forum helped fund a crisis pregnancy center across the street from Planned Parenthood. This investment responds to a negative part of our culture with a positive alternative for hurting women.

I get feedback from wives who say, "I don't know what you're doing in those Forum meetings, but my husband has never prayed like he's now praying with me." That tells me we are becoming a little bit more sensitive, more servant oriented, more focused on spiritual growth and having an eternal impact. By helping each other find our passions, by meeting with them regularly, sometimes playing golf, sometimes eating dinner as couples, I'm learning as much from them as they are from me.

In addition to my Forum, I remain involved with PFA, coaching board members and presidents as we've brought them on. I'm still very active in fundraising and developing new ideas. I work under board chair Bruce Everett and CEO Guy Rogers leadership. The organization isn't dependent on my money or my counsel, but both are appreciated as needed. I've transitioned from being a driving force to being more of a backseat driver. I'm sort of the corporate memory who keeps us connected to our founding vision and history. A new wave of leaders now provide their enthusiasm and fresh vision to try new things like the video forums and podcasts and using social media to get our story into the marketplace. And we're attracting a lot of new people and continuing to grow nationally.

Life tip #83: There is a time to lead and a time to follow.

One of the main reasons God put me on this earth was to create teams that would launch new organizations like Pinnacle Forum. Everything leading up to Pinnacle Forum gave me the spiritual background, the relationship-building experiences and the organizational management experiences that would prepare me for the new assignment from God. Everything that happened in my life prior to 1994 was act one. The start of Pinnacle Forum was act two. Now in act three I'm able to enjoy the fruits of this effort when I meet people who thank me for the impact I've had on them through Pinnacle Forum or another business or ministry I've been part of.

Pinnacle Forum was designed to help Christian leaders move up the ladder of spiritual maturity through the process of finding a relationship with Christ, finding their passion, activating that passion, finding a ministry in line with that passion and then participating in leading a ministry activity that accelerates positive cultural change.

The people we target have leadership capability and a large sphere of influence. We want to help them capture the opportunity to use their influence for Christ wherever they are, then as God calls, to execute in the nonprofit arena at same high level they are doing in their businesses. We want to help them transition from a focus on secular activities to God-centered activities with eternal value, to see their work, their entire lives as service for the kingdom.

We came up with what we called the Four E Strategy to implement our vision. Pinnacle Forum would:

ENCOURAGE leaders to move beyond earthly success to eternal significance (I Thessalonians 5:11).

EQUIP leaders for personal and cultural transformation in confidential peer Forums (Colossians 1:28).

ENGAGE the culture as we discover our God-given purpose and passion for cultural transformation (Matthew 7:7).

EXECUTE intentional strategies for cultural transformation (Ephesians 2:10).

THE PINNACLE FORUM
Where Spiritual Fitness Exercises Yield a Harvest of Personal and Cultural Impact

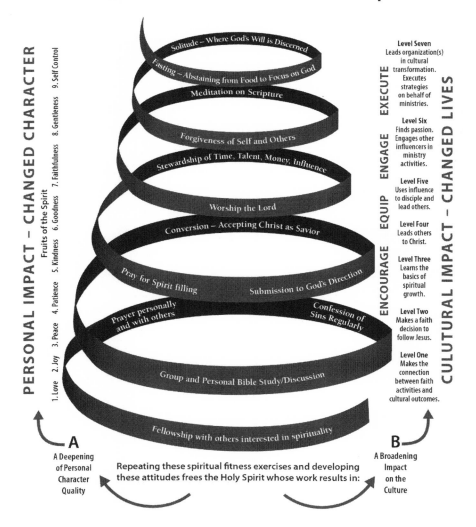

PERSONAL IMPACT – CHANGED CHARACTER

Fruits of the Spirit

1. Love 2. Joy 3. Peace 4. Patience 5. Kindness 6. Goodness 7. Faithfulness 8. Gentleness 9. Self Control

Solitude – Where God's Will is Discerned

Fasting – Abstaining from Food to Focus on God

Meditation on Scripture

Forgiveness of Self and Others

Stewardship of Time, Talent, Money, Influence

Worship the Lord

Conversion – Accepting Christ as Savior

Pray for Spirit filling

Submission to God's Direction

Prayer personally and with others

Confession of Sins Regularly

Group and Personal Bible Study/Discussion

Fellowship with others interested in spirituality

EXECUTE ENGAGE EQUIP ENCOURAGE

CULTURAL IMPACT – CHANGED LIVES

Level Seven
Leads organization(s) in cultural transformation. Executes strategies on behalf of ministries.

Level Six
Finds passion. Engages other influencers in ministry activities.

Level Five
Uses influence to disciple and lead others.

Level Four
Leads others to Christ.

Level Three
Learns the basics of spiritual growth.

Level Two
Makes a faith decision to follow Jesus.

Level One
Makes the connection between faith activities and cultural outcomes.

A
A Deepening of Personal Character Quality

Repeating these spiritual fitness exercises and developing these attitudes frees the Holy Spirit whose work results in:

B
A Broadening Impact on the Culture

Years after we had Pinnacle Forum up and running, we did some research among our Partners and confirmed that when leaders gather in Forums for fellowship, prayer and study, they also increase the time they spend in other spiritual exercises. The average Partner invested 23 percent more time in solitude, 38 percent more time meditating and 12 percent more time in service activities. One year after joining a Forum, Partners report more patience, a deeper sense of inner peace, plus more humility and service orientation. Peer Forums clearly stimulate personal transformation.

Many years later I would summarize and build on the results of our research in the book *You Can Change The World*. It was based on the research Frank Toney and I had done with hundreds of CEOs and seasoned with years of Forum experiences. Here's how the book came about.

During 2010 and 2011 I was recovering from two failed back surgeries. I was wincing and whining a little, and one of my Partners helped me get a grip. "Why don't you write another book? You have nothing else to do." There was a chorus of similar pokes and jabs from the Forum that day. The Holy Spirit connected some other dots of guidance to confirm this course of action.

Dr. Bright had pointed me to the Seven Mountains of Culture as the key spheres where Christian leaders need be present to reshape the culture. I came up with Seven Big Ideas that would equip them to do so. These became the outline for the book. In the introduction I explained what I hoped to accomplish by writing it:

At its very core, this book is about the miraculous power of a Forum of peers where you build relationships that help reshape and execute your vision, values and life passion. The simple truth of this book: You can change the world. But you can't do it alone.

Your confidential Forum of peers is the key to uncovering insights that can renew your energy for life. This is the most powerful leadership development idea I have encountered in my lifetime.

The book unpacks seven big ideas these CEOs have discovered. Their insights will propel you through the same kind of relationship building, personal change and renewal they have experienced. It will help you become an agent of real cultural change.

The Seven Big Ideas or steps up the spiritual development ladder I went on to explore are:

1: Grasp a Big Vision: We can make an eternal difference.
2: Start a Forum of Peers: We are designed with a need for fellowship with each other.
3: Exercise Your Spiritual Muscles: Spiritual fitness prepares us for God's calling.
4: Coach Each Other with Life Stories: We disciple others by living life with others, telling them what God has done.
5: Find Your Service Passion: Over time the Lord places needs on our hearts — wrongs that needs to be corrected.
6: Take a Service "Trial Run": Serving with others, learning from them helps us refine our own plans.
7: Execute a Culture-Change Strategy: Intended investments of our time and money can leverage our influence and make us real culture changers.

Life tip #84: Spiritual exercise leads to cultural change.

We have collected many stories of leaders from around the country who have been impacted by these Big Ideas and who are living out their passion in culture-changing ways. Steve James left the technology industry in 1993 and became an investor and consultant. He got heavily involved in ministries like Homes of Hope, and he's taken hundreds of people to Mexico to build homes for the poor. He also has a ministry mentoring inner city kids in Denver as part of Colorado Uplift. I interviewed one of those young men named Ivan for a book I wrote. "Steve James basically saved my life," Ivan told me. "The way I was going I'd have been dead before I was 18."

Many Partners have a combination of ministry activities going on in their companies and with their families. Some Partners have started their own ministries, while others have come alongside existing ministries or national organizations and helped them have a larger impact by being board members or actively raising funds.

One of our Partners, Rick Stevens, took over leadership of a fundraising project for the YMCA in his community and helped the community raise about $20 million. His whole goal was to put the C—Christ—back in YMCA in that community. Chuck Stetson and Richard Scurry made the cover of *Time* with their Bible as Literature project in the public schools.

These inspiring stories and many more are included in my books and on the PFA website.

I have a story to add. It's an example of Pinnacle Forum in action in our response to Hurricane Katrina, which devastated the Gulf Coast states in August 2005. The storm killed more than 1,800 people, caused more than $81 billion in damage and left thousands homeless. Pinnacle Forum Partners prayed for the hurricane victims, but a small group of us did more.

I led a group of volunteers to help a church in Brookhaven,

Mississippi, a town about 100 miles north of New Orleans overflowing with refugees. Bob Smith from my home church in Cedar Falls traveled with me to Brookhaven to help my cousin, Jamie Oster, and his overloaded volunteers. The church had been swamped by people fleeing New Orleans as the hurricane hit.

We worked quickly to find temporary housing for as many as we could. We bought 14 travel trailers and put displaced families in them rent-free for six months. Christians from Iowa stocked the trailers with linens, kitchen utensils and other items. An RV dealership in Iowa supplied the trailers with no money down. The $300,000 cost was mostly covered by Pinnacle Forum Partners and board members.

I returned to East Haven Baptist Church in 2019 to deliver the eulogy and sermon for my uncle, Donald Oster. An elder met me in the hall to thank me for the help and encouragement "you Iowa boys" brought to this church.

Other past and current board members have also led by example to make an impact by using their influence:

Jerry Colangelo, cofounded the Collaboration for a New Century, a ministry with the vision to see "business, faith, philanthropy and government working together to ensure that individuals and families in vulnerable communities have a quality of life beyond mere existence."

Wes Lane started the Salt and Light Leadership Training (S.A.L.L.T.) program "to train leaders and future leaders of Oklahoma City to be salt and light by imparting an understanding of a biblical worldview . . ."

John Lochner started Legacy Group of America Foundation to "develop enduring relationships that enhance people's lives and leave a legacy of service."

Life tip #85: Passionate leaders can make a big difference.

• • •

MJO Cultural Impact Analysis

Cultural Mountain	Sphere	Participate	Accelerate	Initiate
Family	Family	Prayer Church Read Bible Discuss Live out Time-World Travel Read Bible Stories Christian Camps Christian Schools	Career Testing – Part time College searches Exposure to Industry Leaders Goal Setting Regular Face to Face Naperville Magazine Hudson Pointe **Follow/ Support Kids & Grandkids**	Family Reunion Books- Man of Honor/Woman of Purpose **OSTER PARTNERS** Oster Family History Book Parent/ Grandparent care
Business Religion	Church & Community	Elect 1st Female Mayor Church Elder/ Teacher Bethany Land Gift CF Historic Society KNWS Charity Fund Events -Food -Homeless -Health **Aurora East Support** Christian Schools	Kruger-Oster Track Ministry Trips Phoenix Seminary History's Handful- CRU Invest Time PF Partners **Oster Regent Funding** Hudson Point Development Western Home Hometown Forum Support(CF) CHM CF Chamber Main St. Community Assn Gruber Prison Ministry	Woodstock Rescue Squad Save the Regent Pinnacle Forum Local (2) *Hometowner/Citizen *Oster Farms/Pork Pro **Pinnacle Prairie Development** Established Deacon Ministry Community Prayer Walk Defeat Gambling Campaign CF Development Corporation Vision 2020 CF Chamber
Business Education	Industry	Speeches to: Governors Conferences Bank Conferences Aqri Conferences Finance Conferences Future Conferences Seminars on Land, Futures Serve 250,000 Customers	Consultant to Ford, Ely Lily, etc. Comps Board **Mentor 30 Startup CEO'S** American Graphic Services Naperville Magazine Oster Scholars – Endowed Oster Communications Culture **ELI Mentors**	*Professional Farmers America *Futures Magazine *Future Source- US/Europe *Oster/Dow Jones News *Commodity Price Charts *Parkade Properties **Author 13 Books** **New Mentor Book**
Entertainment Media Government	Nation/World	Norm Burlaug Honor Promise Keepers PFA National Board CRU AIA Banquets Republican Event Home Support Candidates CRU- UN Ministry **Museum of Bible** **YNG (YPO youth)** Chicago Mentoring Program **Pinnacle Forum**	**CRU- Everystudent.com** Russian Pastors Jesus Film 3 Languages Here's Life Board/Sale Support CRU Servants (70) Homes of Hope Edify Opportunity International Coach PF Board/CEO's **Bright Media Foundation** IFI Prison (Colson) **Pure Flix Films** Bible as Literature	Emmaus College Vision 84 Pheasant Hunt Ministries Pinnacle Forum Founding **Pinnacle Forum Board** Oster Charitable remainder Trust Russia/China/Japan Outreaches-CRU Homes for Katrina Victims
Gifts Used		Helps/Teaching	Encouragement/Leadership	Administration/Evangelism

*Entities built and sold

At Pinnacle Forum we encourage leaders to write their Cultural Impact Plan, a strategy to use their time, money and influence for eternal purposes. Carol and I look at our eternal investments annually. Our most recent Cultural Impact Analysis looks like the above.

MJO Cultural Impact

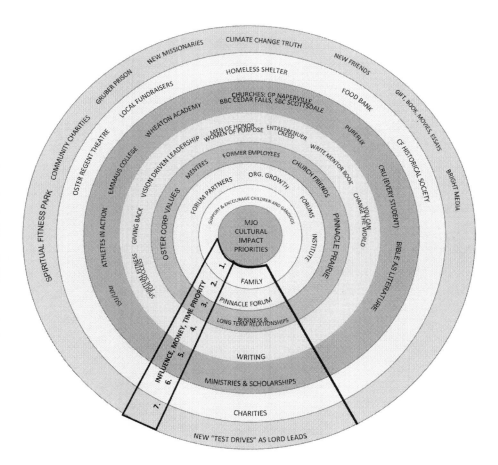

This sphere is one way we look back to remind ourselves where we have invested. And it gives us a glimpse at some of the unmet needs and opportunities we might consider.

• • •

The main reasons for retelling my story are to encourage successful leaders to find a path to true significance by being conduits of God's grace, and to thank my mentors, peers and influencers who have participated in this journey.

I think back to my grandmother who was a conduit of God's grace to me when she explained in a very simple way how to find Christ and walk in the faith. Since then I've had the privilege of doing the same thing with lots of people who have kept the process of spiritual multiplication alive. Today there's a young man named Ivan being a conduit of grace in Denver's inner city because he was impacted by Steve James, who was impacted by Chris Crane, who was impacted by Merrill Oster, who was impacted by his parents and grandparents, peers, mentors and other influencers. There's a string of connectedness that goes from my grandparents' generation to that of my grandchildren, and to the generations they will impact in their lifetimes.

Life tip #86: Influence future generations now.

Ten

Spiritual Fitness
Becoming Dr. Oster

That sounds like an excellent doctoral thesis, Merrill.
Why don't you do it?
—Dr. Frank Toney

In 1994, Carol and I bought a house in Terravita, a new development in Scottsdale, Arizona, for a winter home. One Sunday afternoon Frank and Sarah Toney were walking down the sidewalk past our house. We struck up a conversation, and in the process I asked Frank a question that would change the course of his life and mine. When he told me he was a professor of management and finance at the University of Phoenix, I asked, "Have you ever studied the connection between Christian faith and outcomes in a leader's life?" He was stunned for a minute and finally said, "I never thought of Christianity as a success factor."

Well, I had.

This was the start of an ongoing conversation that led to Frank doing independent research and publishing on the subject, as well as to us working together on several studies and publications. At the time I was doing some of the startup work that launched Pinnacle Forum. I invited Frank to a Good Friday breakfast in Phoenix sponsored by Pinnacle Forum. Frank came home from that breakfast thinking seriously about his eternal destiny. He asked Bill Dodder and me to talk some more about it.

At breakfast in a little restaurant in Cave Creek we explained the Four Spiritual Laws to him: 1. God loves you. 2. Man is sinful and separated from God. 3. Jesus Christ is God's only provision for man's sin. 4. We must individually receive Jesus Christ as Savior and Lord. When we got to the prayer, Frank said, "Let me take a shot at that prayer in my own words." He prayed, "Dear God, I would like to have some of what Merrill and Bill have. I want to walk with Jesus. Amen." That was the start of another level of his spiritual journey.

Bill and I were avid runners. Frank joined us. We ran miles and miles around Lone Mountain and Black Mountain near Cave Creek. We did two marathons, went to the bottom of the Grand Canyon three times and hiked the beautiful mountains of Sedona. On one of the first mornings we jogged together, Frank said, "I don't know how to pray. How do you pray, anyway?" So I said, "Well, why don't you listen to me?" I prayed for two or three minutes, then I gave him an acronym I'd learned for some of the components of prayer. PRAY: Praise. Repent. Adoration. Your needs.

I also directed him to the Lord's Prayer. He never asked me about prayer after that because he could talk to the Lord with the best of us, speaking conversationally right from the heart as we jogged in preparation for our net long run.

Frank had an incredible intellect packaged in a down-home farm boy personality. He was a quick learner, a heck of a student and an award-winning teacher at the University of Phoenix. While he was teaching and doing everything else, he researched and wrote two books on what he was learning about Christianity.

On the way home from a trip down the Grand Canyon, I nudged Frank, "I believe there are certain spiritual exercises that if done diligently are likely to make leaders more successful, more active in their communities and more generous in their giving. Why don't you have some of your graduate students do research on the connection between activities like prayer, fasting and Bible reading and personal and business success?"

I was sitting in the back seat. Frank turned around and returned the nudge, "That sounds like an excellent doctoral thesis, Merrill. Why don't you do it?"

There was a long pause as something stirred in the back of my mind that had been lying dormant for many years. When Carol and I got married in 1962, I was finishing my master's degree. I had enrolled in a PhD program at the University of Wisconsin only to cancel just before classes started. I was newly married and had started a full time magazine job. I also had a part time radio job, and I was selling cookware on the side. It wouldn't have been very wise to start such an arduous program.

I still had an unfulfilled desire to get a doctorate, however, so Frank's nudge and then a push caused me to explore that possibility. A few months later Frank followed up his initial question with an invitation. "Merrill, why don't you come to the University of Phoenix? You can get your degree while running your companies. I'll help you through the process. I'd like to be the chairman of your committee."

Life tip #87: Don't give up your dreams.

So Frank and I began to develop the outline for my dissertation, which resulted in a published study called

"How Spiritual Exercises Correlate with CEO Character Quality and Goal Achievement." On a parallel track, Frank began to gobble up every piece of literature he could find dealing with connections between personal faith and good management practices. This resulted in the book *Biblical Practices: Their Impact on Wealth Accumulation, Happiness and Health*. To a certain extent it followed Frank's own spiritual journey in an academic but easy-to-read format.

I was also on the public speaking circuit at the time and had been asked to speak at the Fellowship Focus Forum conference in San Diego about faith in the workplace. Dr. Bright was on the program as well. Fellowship Focus Forum was a Christian group within YPO. I had been one of its founding members. In preparation I did some survey research among my fellow YPOers. I asked where they were in their faith journey and how it impacted the outcomes in their lives. I asked for details about their financial health, the financial health of their companies, their level of satisfaction, etc.

The data showed that CEOs who consistently made decisions in the context of their religious faith were more satisfied, made more money for themselves and their companies, and gave away more time and money to good causes than people who almost never used religious faith as a determining factor in decision-making. I shared the data with Frank, and he said, "I'd like to write a paper on that." It was later published in the Journal of Leadership Studies under the title "The Leader And His Religious Faith." The results of the study were also reported at the YPO meeting in San Diego.

In a follow-up study conducted with Frank for my doctor-ate we spent a lot of time developing the "instrument" as they called it in the doctoral arena — a questionnaire that generates data that measured the correlation between the activities of faith and the outcomes in business and personal life.

During my doctoral program, begun in 2003 and completed in 2005, I put together a committee that included Frank, Dr. Mike Vandermark from the University of Phoenix and Dr. Terry Perciante of Wheaton College. I interviewed Dr. Henry Brant to get some ideas on how to shape the instrument for my questionnaire. I also spent a day with George Gallup, the famous pollster, and a half day with Darryl DelHousaye who had just completed his own doctorate while being president of Phoenix Seminary and lead pastor at Scottsdale Bible Church.

Life tip #88: Build a strong team of advisors.

This group was like a mentorship team coaching me through this process with Frank as my chairman and the one who influenced me the most. The process gave us a mental model and the research background to talk to people coming into Pinnacle Forum. Frank helped me shape some seminars we conducted with leaders from three or four key cities where Forums were getting started. We formed the Pinnacle Forum Institute and trained 30 leaders at retreats in our timeshare in Sedona's Seven Canyons.

We found statistical evidence for what every well-trained Sunday school kid already knows. If you practice the exercises of the faith such as church attendance, Bible reading, fellowship with other Christians and prayer, you enjoy a better life. You're happier, you make more money, your company makes more money, you have a higher rate of goal satisfaction regardless of what your goals are.

We had a list of 14 spiritual fitness exercises, and we found there was a high correlation between practicing these activities and personal and professional success. My research on 270 CEOs found that CEOs of faith-based companies invested 17 hours per week in spiritual exercises. Those of privately held companies invested 12 hours per week and

CEOs of publicly held companies spent nine and a half hours per week in various spiritual activities.

The spiritual exercises we studied were spiritual conversion, solitude, service, meditation, fasting, fellowship, Bible study, stewardship, worship, confession, submission, prayer, forgiveness and spirit filling.

CEOs who spent the most time on spiritual exercise developed a higher level of humility, honesty and a service-oriented attitude. These three qualities define a servant-leader. Religiously faithful CEOs made better decisions because they heard that small voice of the inner spirit, and they listened to good advice from peers whose voices are sometimes very loud and clear on important issues. My research also showed that CEOs who were more spiritually active achieved a higher level of personal character development and business goal accomplishment.

Religiously oriented decision-makers increased their net worth faster than the nonreligious, in spite of the fact that they gave away more than twice as much money every year. This data pointed to people of faith having something special going for them that others didn't have—what in the Christian tradition is called the Holy Spirit.

Frank was doing his own independent study, gathering information and writing articles. He did another book, *Leadership: It's Biblical Basis*, published in 2002. His work was having an impact on his students. He introduced me to many of them who asked questions about my own journey of faith and my own use of biblical principles in business. Frank and I probably influenced more than a few doctoral projects along these lines.

We were far from alone in our findings. There was a growing body of scientific evidence correlating spiritual exercises with a better quality of life. Professor Peter Glynn of the Department of Management Science and Engineering at Stanford wrote, "Research in medicine, psychology and physiology increasingly connects good outcomes including longer life with spiritual exercises such as forgiveness, prayer, church attendance, fellowship and meditation." Harold Koenig, founder of Duke's Center for Spirituality, Theology and Health, made *Time* magazine with his research suggesting that people who spiritually exercise live seven years longer.

Frank studied and taught servant leadership as modeled by Jesus. He created his own teaching model for leadership he called the Shepherd Model with ideas taken from the 23rd Psalm. He displayed the value of lifelong learning and the ability to learn from peers even while teaching them. He was a pioneer in the use of benchmarking in project management to create standards to gauge progress toward individual goals and overall organizational achievement.

Life tip #89: Spiritual fitness produces goal achievement.

Frank and I developed a very deep friendship. We shared a common background, having both come from farms. We traveled together with our wives. We hunted together. And over the years, the relationship shifted from one where I was mentoring him to one where he was mentoring me through my doctoral program. Eventually we were just peers influencing each another and modeling the kind of relationship we envisioned for Pinnacle Forum Partners.

Pinnacle Forum was a baby organization. It was not even formed when I first met Frank. We helped it grow up together. I took Frank to Pinnacle Forum meetings, and he gave me advice. He was very much a part of my brain trust. The research we did on spiritual fitness both validated and informed what we were teaching in Pinnacle Forum.

People who join Forums spend more time in spiritual fitness exercises, and they accelerate in spiritual growth as well as have an enlarged impact on their cultures.

• • •

Frank Toney went to be with Jesus in August 2018. In remarks I made at his funeral, I celebrated his character and his impact on so many, including myself. He was a good friend who proved to me once again that the true equity in life is in our relationships. Here are a few of my comments from his memorial service:

Frank left several sets of footprints for us to follow. He was curious about what makes leaders tick. He studied CEOs of corporations and wrote many articles that appeared in scientific journals, which future students will reference in their research. Many of his doctoral students at the University of Phoenix went on to lead large organizations. Others wrote articles and books building on his work. He was so respected as a mentor, professor of finance and leadership that his students named him Outstanding Professor of the Year at the University of Phoenix on multiple occasions.

Another set of Frank's footprints remained from his own spiritual journey. As he deepened his knowledge about the Bible and about Jesus Christ, he moved from an inquirer to a serious Christian learner to a devoted follower of Christ and on to become a disciple who would encourage others to follow Christ. We saw this profession of faith, this personal transformation and growth that the apostle Paul talks about in the New Testament. We could see and participate with him in that gradual move from knowing about God, to personally experiencing God's free gift of salvation in Christ, to growing in faith and then to influencing others.

It was a pleasure to be Frank's friend, his student and sometimes his mentor.

Life tip #90: Leave footprints for others to follow.

Eleven

Harvest Time
Watching Lives Be Transformed by Grace

Merrill is a years-long friend and collaborator in transforming the latent energy in American Christianity into active energy.
—Bob Buford, author of *Halftime*

A t this stage in life, Carol and I are focusing on giving back with our investments of time, talent and money. And at the same time, we are enjoying the benefits of previous investments. It is harvest time! We enjoy watching our local church thrive, Pinnacle Forum expand and our grandkids finish college and establish their own homes that will become new conduits of God's grace.

Pinnacle Forum is still our central focus. We enjoy seeing lives being transformed by the hundreds of Pinnacle Forum Partners and the people impacted by the ministries they accelerate. These include the Emerging Leadership Institute (ELI), a mentoring ministry that matches young professionals with business mentors in Chicago. It is a great example of how a group of Partners can execute a strategy that has huge leverage in changing the lives of young influencers. We lend a hand by supporting their effort and annually meeting with the participants to hear their stories.

This year we are watching a crisis pregnancy center building come out of the ground in Aurora, Illinois. It too reflects the work of Pinnacle Forum Partners who have helped raise funds for this new facility that will save hundreds of babies every year and protect their mothers' emotional health.

Pinnacle Forum itself is on the grow and continues to provide new and unique opportunities to invest in cultural change. Despite a budget of under $1 million, we are seeing a wide range of projects started or accelerated by our Partners nationwide, and we log a stream of life-changing stories.

The various ministries of CRU, what used to be called Campus Crusade for Christ, also get a good look from Carol and me every year. We are excited how they are using social media to lead thousands to Christ worldwide through Everyperson.com. And there are many more that God lays on our hearts from time to time. Each year we look at the old favorites and look forward to finding new stories to back and meeting new people who are passionate about their calling. Investing for eternity is such a pleasure.

Over the years we have sponsored more than 50 short-term scholarships for young people who need assistance to remain in college. We endowed the Merrill J. Oster Scholarship at the University of Northern Iowa and Iowa State University. Feedback from these young people is a source of joy and satisfaction.

We have had multiple homes for different seasons of life in Lake of the Ozarks, Lake Geneva and Sedona. But today we focus on summer months in Illinois where we are blessed by the ministry of Derek Webster at Grace Pointe church in Naperville. During winter months we get regular Bible instruction from Jamie Rasmussen at Scottsdale Bible Church in Scottsdale, Arizona. These are incredible servants of God who labor hours each week to help us understand and apply life-giving ideas from Scripture. They are worthy recipients of spiritual and financial investments. Of course our regular visits to Bethany Bible Chapel in Cedar Falls bring us in contact with many friends, peer-mentors and protégés we grew up with while raising our children in our hometown.

It seems like every week someone pops into our lives with a need for direction or a word of encouragement. Carol and I are just playing out what we observed in our homes. Our parents were conduits of God's grace to us. Now we are privileged to be conduits to our children, grandchildren and friends. They, in turn, are conduits of God's grace to us. How we spend our time is as important to us as how we spend our money.

Life tip #91: Time investments are as important as money investments.

Nothing brings us more joy than the time we spend with our children and grandchildren. Our grandparents had a huge impact on us. As a result, we have worked hard to spend quality time with our grandkids. We have spent hundreds of hours doing things with them, not just babysitting but also picking them up from school and taking them hunting or golfing or spending time together at my office or in our swimming pool and rec room.

Carol and I see the fruit of that effort now as our grandchildren become responsible young adults, and as their parents, David and Liz, and Leah and Doug, bring us so much joy as we see the fruits of their lives in family, church and community. The grandchildren help bring us into the world of new social media through texts, emails, FaceTime and other platforms. They inform us on the thinking of their generation and generally keep us young at heart.

David and Leah have served on our company advisory board. They frequently bring insights that inform our business and ministry decisions. Leah has set me straight on up-tempo church music. She overheard me suggest to Pastor John Bell that our drummer was too loud, distracting me from quality worship. I had just completed my discussion with John when Leah stepped in and said, "Dad, there's a service on Tuesday night for old people." That shut me up. However, the next week they put the drummer in a plastic box. Two weeks later they put a lid on the box! Now if they would just take one of his drumsticks away!

Thousands of leaders used to look to me for an opinion on the future price of corn, soy beans and land. Today, I look to David for such information. He is now my counselor, and a good one, with a more healthy attitude regarding risk.

We have six grandkids here on earth. A seventh, Daniel Mark Oster, left this scene the same day he entered. His brief life and unexpected death due to a rare disease had an impact on our family causing us to be more aware of our fragile temporary presence on earth and the value of our relationship with Christ, which brings assurance of eternal life.

Our oldest grandson is Philip, David and Liz's oldest. He works for Guggenheim Securities in Chicago. He graduated from Wheaton College. He is engaged to Sarah Recker (as of January 2019). His brother, Thomas, graduated from Taylor University where he met his wife, Deven. Thomas works for Marcus & Millichap in Oakbrook, Illinois. They attend Spring Valley Presbyterian Church with Philip.

David and Liz's twins, Matthew and Marta, are students at Taylor University in Upland, Indiana. Matthew, a high school soccer player, is now enrolled in business and has a strong interest in creative photography. Marta was a starting goalkeeper in high school but is focusing on her studies. She is entertaining an interest in the mission field. Both attend church in Upland, Indiana.

Our daughter, Leah, and husband, Doug Rippe, have two grown children. Julia Rippe Fifield and her husband, Chase, are pharmacists at Unity Point Hospital in Waterloo. They attend Comdeo Church in Cedar Falls. Derek Rippe is a 2019 Butler University graduate with a double major in music performance and business computing. He is enjoying his first year as a data analyst at Ely Lily in Indianapolis, where he attends Traders Point Christian Church.

Carol and I pray for our children and grandchildren regularly because know they face new and bigger challenges in an increasingly secularized world. We are pleased they have each made a decision to be Christ followers and each is impacting their generation in their own way.

• • •

Sometimes Carol and I enjoy just sitting around the fire, recalling some of the memories we have made together with our kids and grandkids. And when we are with them, they remind us of some of their favorites:

Philip and Thomas like to remind me of the day their Mimi left me in charge of lunch and I fed them yogurt and broccoli. They also recall the day I drove my Lexus SUV through 12-foot weeds to find a deer stand. Since I couldn't see a thing, I rolled the top open and they stuck their heads out and became spotters. Philip was dropped off at his first visit to my Lombard office as a five-year-old wearing a suit to look like Papa. He occupied a cubicle with his name on it, grinning from ear to ear.

Julia and Derek haven't forgotten the trip to the Iowa farm where we explored an abandoned farmstead. The dog we borrowed slipped into a manure pit, and we had a stinky ride home. Nor will they forget a hike I engineered around Estancia Country Club with them and Frank Toney. We took some shortcuts and got a few bites from the sharp underbrush. We stay on the trail these days.

Matthew and Marta recall sliding down a big hill on a snowy day in Aurora and a trip to our Iowa farm where we pulled a toboggan behind the Lexus with their mom Liz and Mimi Carol screaming at the top of their lungs. They got lots of invitations to golf, then lunch with Papa, usually at Subway.

We built memories viewing the Grand Canyon in a helicopter, fishing for Walleyes in Canada, walking the streets of London, hiking in Sedona. There were great times tubing behind the boat on Lake Geneva, golfing in Sedona, Arizona; Walworth, Wisconsin; Bartlett, Illinois, and other spots in the Midwest.

Each grandchild made a few memories hanging out with me at my office. One time I asked four-year-old Derek to hand out a free book to everyone at Christmas time at our Lombard office. He returned with a handful of cash, indicating early on that he might have a career in business. Julia, at age six, mastered naming every state capital on my office wall map and earned a quarter per state.

We have enjoyed teaching grandkids how to drive using the old Pro Farmer van in the open fields. When they were too young to hunt, they rode in the candy-filled van and sat watching the pheasant hunters come our way.

There were many spring breaks with grandkids in Arizona, a few trips to warm beaches and lots of dining at nice restaurants. And everyone made multiple trips to Rawhide, the western town and recreation center near Scottsdale. At the end of a bull-riding exhibition, two-year-old Marta begged, "More bull, Papa! More bull!"

Carol and I have watched an untold number of their

soccer games, tennis matches, basketball and baseball games, concerts, plays and cross country events. What a privilege to watch our grandkids grow up. They certainly have been conduits of God's love to us!

We all benefited from these times together: kids, grandkids and grandparents. In family times the flow of God's grace goes both ways. We bring each other great joy and blessing.

• • •

I thought the Lord had led us back to Iowa in 1969 to start my own business and allow my kids and grandkids to be around my parents and enjoy some of their input as I had with my grandparents. But God had even larger plans in mind. After we arrived in Iowa, I had a wonderful time farming as neighbors with Dad. We enjoyed a whole new relationship as peers. We traded machinery. He gave me advice. But about 18 months after we returned Dad developed a blood clot that was the precursor to cancer. We had some great months together before his conditioned worsened, and he left the scene to be with his Lord on July 6, 1971. It was Dad's 53rd year, our daughter Leah's fifth birthday and easily the worst year of my 31-year-old life.

Mother and I changed roles as Dad's cancer progressed. I was called to be an anchor for mom. I became the go-to person with the doctor. I'm thankful I was there to help with Dad. I did the hospital runs, gave him his shots and was a supporter for my mother as he was fading away.

Dad was a very important mentor to me. I tried to thank him before he passed by saying, "Dad, I want thank you for all the investments you've made in my life." He looked over at me and said, "Well, I didn't do anything. You've been a good son." I heard a similar statement from Ray Routely 10 years later when I thanked him for mentoring me. He said, "Merrill, I've never mentored you. We've just been friends over the years."

In much the same way others have said to me, "Thank you for mentoring me," and I've replied, "I didn't do anything." We might not think we're doing much, yet we are conduits of God's grace. Sometimes it's from one generation to the next. Sometimes it's just from one peer to another.

Moving back to Iowa was a big transition during which I really depended on the Lord. Then my dad died, and I felt the Lord had let me down. I had a strained relationship with God for about nine months. On the one hand I'm the spiritual leader of my family and a leader in the church, so I had to keep a stiff upper lip. But on the inside I'm questioning the Lord. I had fervently prayed that Dad would be miraculously healed. So had a lot of other people. He wasn't.

Only later did my friend and mentor Ray Routely and others help me come to realize that I'd set my expectations, but God is sovereign. I needed to adapt to his plan as opposed to trying to pray God into mine. That little breakthrough was an important step in enlarging my faith. It helped me understand more about who God is and how he works in people's lives.

I don't remember exactly what Ray Routely or Bob Smith Sr. or Ernie Matthias or Howard Dunkerton or Paul Sapp said to me. They were just there for me with an open Bible, open minds and open hearts that poured out love as I was mourning Dad's loss. That's what Christian mentors do. **Life tip #92: Set expectations by God's standards.**

● ● ●

I have cruised into semiretirement with no staff, only a few consulting development experts, accountants and lawyers. I am thinking about slowing down, but I still have some unfinished business.

As an active board member, leader, coach and founder of Pinnacle Form, I invest a few hours every week, either nationally or locally. Once or twice a year I give a speech to help a ministry or to celebrate the life of a peer. I help facilitate a Pinnacle Forum at our Stonebridge Country Club where I meet with nine other guys. I also do some one-on-one mentoring.

I have my hand (and billfold) deeply in Pinnacle Prairie, a 720-acre development between Cedar Falls and Waterloo I created from farmland acquired over the years. It is the largest planned multiuse development in Iowa. It is reshaping south Cedar Falls from cornfields into a thriving community. It will be a few more years before it's completely filled in, but it's creating a wonderful lifestyle for the 1,500 people living there already. We have Unity Point hospital, some churches and several retail operations as well as the Cedar Falls Public Safety facility, headquarters for the police and fire departments.

An anchor business is Menards and an anchor ministry is Western Home, one of the most sophisticated retirement centers in America. Fareway Foods just opened a beautiful grocery store. Creating a new community brings real joy as we watch Cedar Falls expand where corn once grew. Interestingly, Tori Lockard is our lead sales person. She's the daughter of Ken, a man I mentored and the granddaughter of Wendell, a man who mentored me.

I'm also involved in Hudson Pointe, a 512-acre farm which is a proposed real estate development with our son David and other partners in Oswego, Illinois. There I hunt geese and dove while waiting for Illinois political conditions to improve.

Mike Schoppe is not only a hunting buddy but also a land

planner on our development projects. I am frequently joined on goose hunts by Mel Tradeau, a Stonebridge neighbor to whom I was introduced by Joe Bernardo, our former CEO at *Futures* magazine. Joe also hunts a few times in our Pit, Palace or Den, as we call our hunting hideouts!

I hike a mountain a few times each winter, hunt geese in the fall, golf whenever the sun shines, swim when it's hot and bike when I need a change of pace. In each of these activities, there is usually a friend doing life with me. Sometimes they have a positive impact by encouraging me. Occasionally I probably encourage them.

At this time, I am planning a company reunion for our Pro Farmer and Futures family. It will be great to renew the many wonderful friendships made while starting and building companies. How we all treasure our friendships and memories created during the past five decades!

Speaking of friendships, four of us in Cedar Falls/ Waterloo business peers are planning our 29th annual get-together for three days of golf and laughter. Larry Reed, John Peterson and Mark Baldwin have joined me to renew our friendship on the golf course. Each of us has been through at least one major family or business crisis since our first outing. As with our Pinnacle Forum Partners, we have learned the value of having close, caring friends, especially in times of crisis.

• • •

This represents the seventh and final draft of this manuscript. I started dictating one-hour memory dumps each week starting in October 2018 between goose hunts. Sometimes I talked to Mike Hamel's recorder from my phone with one eye on the sky searching for geese.

It's now February 2019. We have had two interruptions. On January 3, I received word that my dear uncle Donald Oster passed at age 88. We had been texting and calling twice a month for years. I officiated at his funeral and reconnected with my first cousins Dale, Daryl, Creig, Jamie and Chris Oster.

Then on Saturday, February 2, just three weeks ago, I got the shocking news that my brother, Larry, my only sibling, had passed into eternity at age 76. Half of my heart is still weeping, while the other half jumps for joy. So here I sit, mourning by writing. These two dear ones are walking the streets of gold, so, in general, I rejoice.

Looking forward, there are new golf courses yet to conquer, new assignments from God to experience, new friends to make, new family memories to create, new restaurants to explore, new ministries to accelerate, new people to nudge toward cultural change and new ways to advance the cause of Christ by helping build the kingdom.

As Dr. Bill Bright said so frequently, "The best is yet to come."

Twelve

Eternal Conduits of Grace
Accelerating the Good in Others, Forever

Merrill's example of leadership has had such a big impact on me. I learned many things from him that I've used as CEO of my own company and of Opportunity International. I've given up the CEO role now, but I still follow Merrill's example as a mentor.
I've done a great deal of mentoring and I love doing it.
— Chris Crane, former CEO of Opportunity International and Founder of Edify

I asked my friend and fellow author, Mike Hamel, to interview some of the men and women I have served with over the years. They say I influenced them, but in every case I can tell you each one brought a blessing into my life as well. Years after I'm gone, the impact of these friends will still be felt on generations to come. That's how conduits of God's grace become conduits to others who become, well, you get it.

Take Jerry Carlson, for example. He showed me how to integrate faith and journalism. His writing took mine to a higher level. He laid the tracks for every editorial project we launched at a level beyond what I could have done.

He started his own company and has played a key role in his church.

Darrell Jobman helped me dig out from under a workload when I overcommitted. His steady demeanor during crises calmed my own nerves. He started his own consulting firm and continues to serve generously.

Rex Willmore learned every function I performed, then he took it to a higher level. He had the courage to tell me when I was dead wrong. He left Oster after 23 years and started his own freelance business. There never was a better peer counselor and friend.

Larry Graham could charm an audience and improve on every good seminar idea I could think of. His care for people was central to creating a servant leadership culture in the company. His consulting firm to large farmers has impacted thousands of leaders.

Dan Manternach brought fresh energy to our efforts and had a unique ability to hold an audience in the palm of his hand. His presence freed me to refocus our company. His enthusiasm fueled us all. He still gets lots of invitations to fill important platforms.

Mike Walsten's example of consistently getting high-quality analysis to our readers and meeting deadlines helped us set high productivity standards. He knew how to train reporters to get lots of market-moving news quickly. He was the longest-serving Pro Farmer employee.

Ron Michaelson provided us with a reminder that God has a sense of humor. His willing attitude to drop what he was doing to start something else was an example to all of us. He still offers his lending hand to me and others with a servant's heart.

Milo Hamilton brought a deeply thoughtful, sometimes academic, approach to his work. He has always been quick to give others credit. He has started a few businesses of his own, including Firstgrain, which tracks the world's rice markets. He is also impacting leaders by recruiting them to Pinnacle Forum.

Sandy Golz provided our team with a "get it done right the first time" approach. Her command of spelling and grammar caught lots of my mistakes before they were printed.

Chris Crane brought Wall Street savvy to a bunch of farm-boy entrepreneurs. He showed me a Christlike level of humility. His ministry startup will serve future generations.

Steve James led both Chris and me in using financial analytical skills, combined with integrity and honesty, in deal-making situations where these qualities are usually in short supply.

Moving outside the company to the broader Christian community, Dave Glock opened passages of Scripture as a platform preacher that had a big impact on my spiritual growth. Then working with him as a leader at Emmaus Bible College, he brought an openness to new ideas that was refreshing.

In the local community, Larry Reed's outspoken enthusiasm for the Lord as CEO of an auto dealership helped me find a peer, a partner in similar purposes and a fellow encourager.

Ron Kiewiet, a friend from grade school, was a hunting buddy who taught me how to shoot a gun and skin a rabbit. We learned to have fun in the fields our dads farmed and have never lost touch.

Carolyn Hamrock challenged me to help save the Regent Theatre in Cedar Falls. I threw her name in the hat when the *Jesus* film project needed a fundraising strategist. She helped locally and globally.

Bill Dodder helped us build Pinnacle Forum on solid biblical principles. Praying with Bill helped me keep my focus on depending on the Lord, not my own wisdom. He has poured his life into hundreds of others, probably thousands, and is still at it!

It is interesting how God has worked to bring blessing into my life from young men I apparently influenced when they were just kids. Now a highly accomplished adult, Ken Lockard has advised me in areas where his experience shed light on how to proceed in real estate affairs. What encouragement comes from watching him grow as a Christian businessman. His daughter, Tori Lockard, plays a big role in our Pinnacle Prairie sales effort.

Bob Smith Jr., like his dad, has similarly given me financial advice and used his relationships in our hometown to make progress at Pinnacle Prairie. His incredible sensitivity to God's leading in decision-making continues to be a blessing and example to me.

Tim O'Conner has spent an hour a week studying Scripture with me. We mentor each other with our new insights from God's word. He will mentor many others in his circle of influence.

Gene Redlin helped me turn a company around. We prayed, laughed and cried together. Since then he has started churches and influenced thousands through his spiritual blogs.

Bruce Everette has been leading the Pinnacle Forum America board. I'm learning from him how to bring out the best in a board. He is a great leader with multiple ministry involvements.

These men and women have truly been conduits of God's grace to me and many, many others.

FRIENDS FROM 18 TO 80
by Jerry Carlson

Merrill and I were journalism students at Iowa State. He was a dynamo on the radio. I worked in print because I think more slowly. I don't think I ever saw him walk. He was always running. He had tremendous energy. He was a strong writer and a very independent guy, even then. He wanted to study what he wanted to study and do his own thing. I was a few years older and became Merrill's pledge father at FarmHouse fraternity. We had a really close friendship and a wonderful bond. I admired him greatly. Still do.

Several years later when I was in Philadelphia working at *Farm Journal*, he called me out of the blue and said, "I'm starting off on my own and am looking for a second person to join my editorial team. Would you be interested?" He later came out to visit Jill and me in Pennsylvania. He asked straight out, "Where are you spiritually?" We had a rather extended talk about what Christianity was and where my faith was placed. Did I really know what the Gospel meant? Did I trust in Jesus totally? Merrill did not want to be unequally yoked in a partnership as far as fundamental beliefs were concerned. If there's any one thing that sustained our friendship and partnership through awful things – my shortcomings in particular – our shared faith was it. I failed him on one occasion that cost him $80,000 to correct. In all our years together, we had disagreements, but we never had a battle.

To be a financial partner was one thing; to be an employee was a different ballgame. Faith wasn't required to be an employee. Merrill valued integrity and capability. If you showed neither, you were gently asked to go find a better opportunity elsewhere. I did not once see Merrill discriminate against anyone on the basis of faith. But If you goofed off, cheated, did anything like that, he was very decisive. You were gone. Everybody knew this and appreciated it. I think that was foundational to us having the kind of work atmosphere where you could trust your buddy. You knew your associates were competent. They were carrying their share of the weight or a little bit more. We did not require a lot of supervision, which meant Merrill could explore other opportunities, which he did.

Merrill was always looking for new enterprises. His interest in commodity trading led him to focus more and more on that area. I was big into computers. My master's thesis was on computer-based writing and editing. I pushed hard to get us up and running on the internet. Merrill backed the idea, and as a result we developed one of the first electronic news delivery systems in agribusiness.

We had one of the first photo typesetters in Cedar Falls. I wanted to expand the typesetting operation and pushed to take in outside work. When this began to interfere with getting our own publications out, Merrill said, "This isn't focusing on what we really do." At that point I had so much ego involved that I replied, "Well, if you don't want to have it in-house, I'll move it down the street on my own." That was stupid on my part. I wound up selling that business at a loss after a few years and focused on editorial work and web development. I developed the first Pro Farmer website and some other websites within the company. That was my passion — getting the news out quickly and correctly to serve farmers.

Pinnacle Forum was one of the fruits of Merrill being able to do what he wanted. He used his considerable talents and courage and connection to Bill Bright and other wonderful people to do something far beyond just making money.

"It's all about relationships between people," Merrill would say, "It's about trust and friendships. If you don't have those, you don't really have what I would call a company." And Merrill lived it. I admire that. It's an inspiring thing to be associated with somebody with that degree of caring.

WE CHANGED THE WORLDVIEW OF FUTURES
by Darrell Jobman

I was farm editor for the *Waterloo Career* and had received several barbs from Merrill because my columns sometimes repeated coffeeshop conversation about nasty futures speculators who were ripping off the farmer. He sent me a letter that essentially said hogwash. Years later after getting to know Merrill, I wrote a book about him in which I documented how he was among the first to communicate to a wide audience the value of futures, addressing farmers initially and later reaching a much broader business audience.

His message to farmers was basic: "Up and down the railroad tracks and highways in the rural America stand huge storage facilities. They are owned by grain companies, but as farmers we have paid for them by not understanding marketing our grain. Learn to use future's markets to know when to sell in futures and when to sell in cash." That message carried new hope for farm families, and coming at a time of significant economic events made Merrill a popular leader in the effort to change the economic landscape of rural America through the creation of viable, business-oriented family farming enterprises.

When Merrill started ComCo, the business took off and he was getting overwhelmed and looking for help. He hired me part time in 1969, and three years later I became his first full time employee. Then Merrill and Jerry Carlson started Professional Farmers of America, pretty much out of their own personal finances. Merrill was also farming at the time. We worked well together. In newspapers you have a lot of space to fill, so my habit was to write long. Merrill would whack it down. He was a great editor, and he would smooth it down to where it was half as long but said twice as much.

As an employer he was very good at looking out for his employees. He was interested in us and how we were doing. Coming from a little farm in Nebraska, I'd never thought about a 401K or anything like that, but Merrill set that up for us. He had great foresight.

Pro Farmer built a solid reputation over the years. We had seminars around the country and would even arrange trips for farmers overseas like the one I went on to South America. Instead of just being an information service, we became a network of farmers. We were kind of a big happy Pro Farmer family.

As Pro Farmer got bigger, Merrill decided to set up his own news source. That was part of the reason he bought *Commodities* magazine in 1976 and named me the editor. At the same time, he started doing charts for farmers. There was always Commodity Research Bureau, but again Merrill decided we could do it better, so he started Commodity Price Charts in 1977. For farmers it was a revelation to pay attention to market movements based on charts. Then we got into data services and delivering information electronically.

By the end of the 1970s, 32,000 high-income farmers representing more than 50 percent of America's annual agricultural income were relying on *Pro Farmer* for timely data on market trends. Another 65,000 commodity traders and industry leaders looked to *Oster's Commodities*, later *Futures* magazine, for risk management information and direction.

I became the chief operating officer and then president of the company. Titles were not that important at Oster. All a title really said was, here's what you're responsible for. In terms of perceived value or contribution to the company, we were all more peers than having a certain pecking order. What was important to Merrill were spiritual values. They were built into the culture of the company. You could see

Merrill as the example of the culture he believed in. He was someone you wanted to associate with — the kind of person who had convictions and who showed them by what he did for his employees and the farmers and future's traders he was trying to help. It was important for me that his attitude was based on a spiritual foundation.

Merrill had great vision for what would work and an instinct for when something had reached its peak. What they say when you're in trading is, "Don't let profits slip away." For example, he pretty much got out of the hog business at one of the peaks in the mid 1990s. He also sold *Futures* magazine and Pro Farmer with a sense of timing that was uncanny.

I'm very grateful for all Merrill did for me. Not just as an employer but as a person and a friend.

Point Man through It All
by Rex Wilmore

I was working for *Farm Journal* magazine in Philadelphia. My close friend Jerry Carlson had left there to help Merrill start *Pro Farmer*. When they were ready to expand their editorial staff, I got a call from Cedar Falls. I went out, attended what I believe the first seminar they ever did and was so impressed that I was hooked.

I did the *Pro Farmer* newsletter and anything else I could do to help. In a few years, I got into direct mail, and the material Peter Cornell and I wrote outperformed the package from a high-powered direct mail consultant. After that I became the writer of all direct mail pieces for several years. I also did some marketing and operations. Whenever something needed to be done, I would hold up my hand and say, "Maybe I could do that." It was one of the most fun and challenging times of my whole life.

The culture was innovative. Pretty much everybody was encouraged to try almost anything they wanted to. What kept it interesting was that Merrill would occasionally come in and say something like, "Hey, I bought *Commodities* magazine today. We're going to put out the next issue in three weeks." Well, we'd never done that before, but three weeks later we put one in the mail. There were times when Merrill might have gotten a little autocratic, and that could be stressful.

Merrill was very good at generating ideas. One time on a trip to Hawaii he put together for about 150 farmers, we sat up all night and designed a new publication that became *CornPro*. And on the way back, again overnight, we worked on the direct mail to launch it a couple weeks later.

Part of my role became talking Merrill out of some of his ideas or trying to modify them so they became a little more reasonable for the staff. Everybody worked long hours when needed. We had a lot of great people who were willing to go the extra mile.

I had a very serious medical issue in 1976. I ended up spending several days in the hospital and then another six months of rehab and recovery. Merrill, Carol and their kids were totally supportive of our family. There was never any question of reducing my pay while I was out or anything like that. It was just, "You're coming back, and we'll see you as soon as you can. Don't overdo it; we're praying for you."

Mentoring was a part of the company-wide culture. Jerry Carlson mentored everybody. I mentored quite a few people myself, both in Cedar Falls and in the Lombard office. Merrill mentored me by challenging me and by mostly constructive criticism. There were some people that didn't take to that very well but then they tended not to last very long, either.

There were so many things that were good. We had an annual event for many years called the Spring Fling. The staff and families would go to a resort-type area for a long weekend. We pretended to work some, but basically it was a chance to get together and bond as families. I've never known another organization that did something like that.

Another great perk Merrill provided to the management staff were the vacation homes he had on the Lake of the Ozarks in Missouri. Staying there was a marvelous perk. And one year for Christmas, Merrill gave some executives 1,000 miles of airtime in his Cessna Twin. Tom Pierson and I put our miles together and took our wives to New Orleans.

Merrill bought Commodity Communications Corp in the early '80s. Because I helped with some of the technical aspects of the negotiations, I became Merrill's point man. After we had been through three managers, we both realized the only way to get control of that organization was if I moved to the Lombard office. I rebuilt and streamlined parts of the organization, and it turned into a pretty nice little business.

I left Oster after 23 years. I got a good severance package and went into freelance work. Sometimes I had Merrill for a client. We are still friends; he's been important in my life. I'm looking forward to the Oster reunion planned for this summer.

STILL DOING WHAT WE LEARNED AT *PRO FARMER*
by Larry Graham

I first met Merrill in Hot Springs, Arkansas at a meeting of the American Soybean Association. I was working for *Prairie Farmer* magazine at that time. Merrill and I hit it off. We both belonged to the American Agricultural Editors Association and would see each other at annual meetings. We developed a friendship over the years.

In 1975 I was the executive secretary of the Illinois Pork Producers Association in Des Moines when Merrill called to offer me a job. My wife said, "Forget it. I'm not living where it's colder than it is here." But Merrill's a charmer, and he got us to Cedar Falls to look around. I knew how busy he was, but he spent the whole day with us. I was impressed. And my wife was moving forward to being ready. So we decided to take the job and moved to Cedar Falls.

We enjoyed 10 years there. It was the best job I've ever had. It was so much fun. Merrill and I would drive out in the middle of a cornfield sometimes and just brainstorm about business. We were so excited about the future and what we were doing.

Merrill had it all together. He's the smartest person I've ever met. He's a strong Christian and very successful businesswise. He's the best negotiator I've ever seen, in a good way. He was tough. He was straightforward. He always knew what he wanted to get done. He was also a great speaker. I tried to be like him in terms of my speaking ability. I never got there but I picked up a lot by watching him.

I was originally hired to write a pork newsletter, but Merrill asked me to head the Pro Farmer Institute. We put on seminars and meetings for farmers all over the country. One lesson I learned from my very first seminar with Merrill is still with me. I was in charge of the meeting and something came up that meant we were going to be delayed. I announced we would go longer than normal. But Merrill stood up and said, "Wait a minute. We're going to keep this meeting on time." I've never forgotten that. I've been putting on meetings since 1975, and that's a rule I've never broken. You start on time; you end on time.

I also learned what I call empathy from him. He felt for his audience and wanted them to go home with something to help them be better at their jobs. He wanted them to feel really important about what they were doing as professional farmers. They were feeding the world.

Merrill had a very warm personality. He was easy to follow—the kind of person you wanted to be around. And he had a great sense of humor. That's partly what made it so much fun to work and travel with him. At the same time, he was clear about what he expected.

I had only been there a short time when he called me into his office and said, "I'd like you to do this." I don't remember what it was. And I said, "I'm not sure I feel comfortable doing that." And he said, "I'm not asking if you're comfortable about it. I'm asking if you can do this job." He said it in a kind way. I didn't take offense, but I knew exactly what he was talking about. He was asking me to do something he knew I was qualified for, and he didn't want to hear an excuse. I've never forgotten the lesson: Do what you're capable of doing. When he hired me, he gave me the impression that I could do anything. I still have the letter I got from him detailing what he expected of me and what he thought I was capable of.

The Osters had a place at Lake of the Ozarks in Missouri, and they shared it with some of the families from work. Frequently Merrill, Carol, David and Leah would be there, and we'd do things together. He had a GMC motor home called the Green Machine. Several of us were allowed to use it on occasion. My family has great memories of the Lake and the Green Machine. My kids have a high regard for Merrill and Carol. They were very generous.

Years after I left Oster, my wife and I started our own business. We put on meetings for large farmers advising them on marketing strategies, and I've been able to use what I learned from Merrill. The business has done well. We're fortunate to have gotten acquainted with some of the best farmers in the world, and we count many among our lifelong friends. These are the same people that Merrill started Professional Farmers of America to help.

FROM PIGPEN TO PRO FARMER PLATFORM
by Dan Manternach

I became aware of Professional Farmers of America before I ever met Merrill. When I returned to the family farm after graduating from Iowa State in 1973 with a degree in journalism, I started getting these newsletters from an outfit called Professional Farmers of America. Later, I went to Illinois to manage a hog farm. I met Merrill at a Pro Farmer seminar in Peoria, Illinois. We talked and he invited me to Cedar Falls to look at his operation.

I took him up on the offer and met with Jerry Carlson, another Iowa State alum who had first contacted me about a job with Pro Farmer. They wanted to develop a sense of professionalism among farmers, and this very much appealed to me. I was hired to edit a newsletter called *CornPro*, which was a spinoff of the *Pro Farmer* newsletter. Merrill was very sensitive to feedback from subscribers and the feedback he was getting was, "You covered six commodities, but I only care about corn and beans." So he started a newsletter called *CornPro* for those who wanted more detail about only the corn market. Later he did the same thing with *PorkPro*.

One of the things that made *Pro Farmer* a cut above the competition was that their advice tended to be wishy-washy whereas Merrill's advice in *Pro Farmer* was quite specific. That was something new. The *Pro Farmer* newsletter would say, "Sell ten percent of your anticipated production when December corn hits overhead resistance at $2.25 on the charts." And speaking of charts, those were among Merrill's other innovations. He launched the first agricultural publications that introduced farmers to charts and the use of technical analysis of price trends.

When the editor for the *Pro Farmer* newsletter left in 1979, I got the job. I also did some of the seminars with the

Pro Farmer Institute. Merrill had created the Pro Farmer Institute that offered seminars on topics like marketing and land buying for farmers during their off-season.

Part of what drew me to Pro Farmer was that my Christian faith and heritage were very important to me. I remember at the Peoria seminar that when we broke for lunch, Merrill gave the blessing in front of the whole crowd. That impressed me. And in my interview, he asked about my own faith journey.

Merrill made frequent references in his speaking engagements to his faith. During a break at a Pro Farmer seminar, I overheard a farmer say to him, "I really like these seminars. I get a lot out of them for my business. But I get a little weary of the way you wear your religion on your sleeve." I'll never forget Merrill's response: "Oh, I'm sorry it shows just on my sleeve. I wanted it to show all over."

Another thing about Merrill that really impressed me was that when he was wrong, he would admit it. There are a lot of chief executives who strictly abide by the "never let them see you sweat" mantra. When Merrill made a mistake, he was not too big to admit it to the rest of the staff. I've always respected him for that.

Our company meetings would begin with prayer. And Merrill would say things like, "Thank Jesus for that," or, "Didn't expect it to go that well. That was a God thing." These weren't throwaway lines. They were definitely by design and part of the corporate culture Merrill wanted everybody to be aware of.

Sometime in the 1980s, Merrill was approached by a Christian organization called Food for the Hungry with a request to promote their cause to our membership. In typical Merrill fashion, he checked out how efficient FFH was in terms of dollars and even went a step further. He took Merlyn Vandekrol and me and another associate on a trip to

Guatemala to observe FFH's work firsthand. We visited poor Mayan villages where FFH taught farmers how to reduce spoilage and how to get clean drinking water. We ended up openly promoting FFH in the *Pro Farmer* newsletter itself.

I know that a lot of the success I've had in my career, even after *Pro Farmer*, I owe to Merrill for what he modeled and taught me about serving and being of value to others.

WE GREW UP TOGETHER, PROFESSIONALLY AND IN FAITH
by Mike Walsten

I was at *Farm Journal* magazine in Philadelphia. Jerry Carlson had gone from there to help start *Pro Farmer*. He recruited me in '75 to work on their *PorkPro* and *CornPro* newsletters. I found a good atmosphere to work and learn in and a lot of camaraderie. Merrill's Christian faith was very much in the forefront. So was Jerry's. This was an attraction for my wife and me. I was a Christian but not a very strong one at the time. Having bosses who were so out front with their faith was unusual, but I came to appreciate and really enjoy it as the years went on.

Their beliefs were so much a part of what we did. At Pro Farmer seminars, there would be prayer before the meals and thanking the Lord for all the blessings we'd been given. Merrill would give presentations that showed how his faith and work all came together in his life. He talked about developing life goals and trusting God to provide direction and support going forward. He spoke of having a faith in Jesus Christ and a personal relationship with him, which brought comfort and support to a lot of people. This was in the '80s when farmers were going through tough times.

Merrill and his companies faced a lot of stress and difficulties like everyone else in agriculture at that time. He was very vocal about saying, "This is all yours, Lord, it's not mine. Direct me in what we need to do." I found this dependence on God very inspiring in terms of my growth and my commitment to the company and to Merrill.

Merrill and Jerry and other executives mentored by example. Merrill was actively involved, but not always on a daily basis. He would evaluate the publications and give us some constructive criticism that sharpened our focus editorially.

I also watched what Merrill was doing in the community. One of the most significant things I noticed was his commitment to revitalize downtown Main Street. It was really suffering in the '80s because of the recession. Businesses didn't want to be there. The block between First and Second Street was anchored by the Regent Theatre, but it was closed and just sitting there. Merrill's efforts to restore what became the Oster Regent Theatre really set things in motion. Today there are restaurants, stores and four-story apartment buildings with retail shops on the first floors. You can't find a parking place!

Toward the end of the '90s, Merrill sold several of his businesses. I transitioned back to Pro Farmer, which was bought by *Farm Journal*. I never left the building but this ended my formal association with Merrill.

His influence on my life was very important. Seeing a Christian man staying true to his faith in his business life really affected me and stirred a commitment in me to build a strong Christian life and pass biblical values on to my children and my grandchildren. I've always appreciated that.

RADIO VOICE FINDS A HOME
by Ron Michaelson

I started working for Merrill in 1980 at Pro Farmer and did various jobs until 2002. He was quite a dynamo. He ran about a dozen businesses and had the largest hog operation in Iowa for a time. He farmed thousands of acres, traded commodities, wrote 10 books, preached sermons at church, ran marathons. The only thing he didn't do was juggle, and maybe he did that when I wasn't looking. He's an amazing entrepreneur who was able to capitalize on opportunities.

Merrill set a high example. We all wanted to emulate him. He ran his business in a unique way. Oster Communications was a very unusual place to work. It was pretty hard to get fired. People did, but you had to really work at it. Merrill's philosophy was to hire good people. If they didn't work out in one area, he would move them around until they found something they could do really well. I got moved around quite a bit.

I was a different kind of an animal, and Merrill groomed me into something useful. He was primarily interested in hiring other journalists who were farm boys or girls. I was a farm boy; I grew up about 10 miles from Merrill, but I'd gone to a liberal arts school and become a farm broadcaster.

In my first week I was still in orientation and the editorial director came to me and said, "You're going with Merrill in the airplane to Peoria. He's got a speech, and he's sick as a dog." I got on this little six-seater airplane and we talked the whole trip. It was probably the first time I got to share with him about my faith. I'd only been a Christian for a year. He shared some of his experiences and also coached me on what to say at the event.

"Just get up and tell them why you came to Pro Farmer," he told me. "Tell them how you feel about the importance of farm land and agriculture, and be upbeat about it." And that's what I did. That was my introduction to Pro Farmer. Hey, get on the airplane with Merrill and go do his seminar for him. I eventually ran the seminar department and did a lot of that sort of thing over the years.

Everything was done with excellence and decorum. It was so much fun to work in a place where there were no dirty jokes or bad language or flirting with women. It was a kind of place that if you weren't a Christian you got a very good impression of what Christians were like. There was recognition at five years of service and up. At 10 years you got a fancy gold watch. Then at 20 years, Merrill gave vacation trips to Europe or wherever. People stayed at Oster a long time because they liked the place.

In 1935, there were about seven million farmers in the US. That number dropped to about two million by 1990. Many of those were lost in the early '80s. There were 500 auctions a month, I remember, throughout the Midwest. We lost at least half our customer base, and things were tough for Merrill. He had a lot of land and was personally being impacted by the low commodity prices. He was in way over his head, but he never asked us to take a pay cut. He sold any asset he could find, either personal or business. He made whatever sacrifices he could to keep us together. It gets me teared up right now just thinking about it.

There's one area where it really touched me personally working for Merrill. I'd only been there about a year when I was in a very bad accident. I was off work for almost two months, but I got my paycheck every two weeks. There was nothing in the employee handbook that said he had to do that; he just did it. When you're a young guy just starting out and the owner of the company takes care of you this way, that's got a lot of impact.

I know he did this for other people as well. My friend

Merlyn Vandekrol was an important person at Oster Communications. He got colon cancer several years ago and passed away. Merlyn told me as he was dying that Merrill was continuing to pay him. I think Merrill even took care of Merlyn's wife for a while afterward. This impacted me as someone who was close to Merlyn and who knew things that Merrill didn't publicize.

Whenever anybody says anything about Merrill Oster, I go, "The greatest guy I could ever work for." If they'll take time to listen, I've got lots of stories like this to prove it.

THE CONDUIT BETWEEN BUNKER AND MERRILL
by Milo Hamilton

I was looking for something to do after leaving the University of Minnesota and a friend who wrote for a magazine said, "Go talk to those *Pro Farmer* people. They're doing something different." I was interested in agriculture and the markets but didn't want to stay in academia. I didn't want to go back to my dad's farm, either, so I called Merrill and he had me come for an interview. We sat across from each other and he asked, "What do you want to do?" And I said, "I want to learn everything I can and then go out and compete with you." He thought that was kind of humorous, and that's how it began.

I was the only employee who wasn't trained in journalism at the time. Merrill gave me on-the-job training. He went after my material like a coach with a young recruit. I learned a lot about how to do what he did. I was inspired by his role as a businessman. He made me to want to start my own business. And I wasn't the only one. There were others. This was a way of life for Merrill. He reached out and helped people like me to be better at what we did. He seemed to take pride in mentoring me and others. He cared about us and wanted us to have the same opportunities he had. He helped his staff as well as his customers. He was a very unusual man in that regard.

Merrill taught me well enough that I've got my own thriving business. It's on a much smaller scale than his but doing the same thing. I still call Merrill from time to time. He's like an advisor at a distance. He's a person that I've always trusted and when he gives me advice, I think a lot about it.

At a Pinnacle Forum event in Chicago years ago, Merrill came up to me and said, "None of this would have happened without you, Milo. You connected me with Bill Bright and he and I started Pinnacle Forum and here you are, a member in the very program you played a role in starting." He reminded me of the time he sent me to interview Nelson Bunker Hunt. I was the only person who got an interview during the whole silver fiasco. I told Mr. Hunt that he might want to talk to my boss, Merrill Oster, because he might be interested in helping with the *Jesus* film. At that time I didn't have a personal relationship with the Lord, but I knew where Merrill stood since he was very outspoken about his faith.

Mr. Hunt did call Merrill and invite him to LA where he was finishing up with the *Jesus* film. It went on to be one of the most viewed movies in the history of mankind. While in LA Mr. Hunt introduces Merrill to Dr. Bill Bright. The two of them went on to create Pinnacle Forum to encourage people with influence to have an impact for the culture for the kingdom of God.

So even before I knew Jesus on a personal basis, he was making use of me. I finally found the Lord myself in 1999 after I'd left Merrill's organization. Merrill looked me up and got me into a Pinnacle Forum group. It has transformed my personal life and my business life. It's inspired me to redo my whole business.

Words can't really describe what I think about Merrill. He can be gruff and tough at times, but he shows with his actions how much he loves and cares for others. There aren't many people like that I've come across.

Always Ready for the Next Challenge
by Sandy Golz

I was hired as Merrill's executive assistant in 1984. I had been working at the university and Oster Communication had an entirely different culture from education. In talking with people who worked in other businesses, I learned it was a very different culture from what they knew as well. It was a very Christian-based organization, and Merrill placed great emphasis on that in his hires and in his activities. We always had a prayer at meetings. It was a fast-paced place to work, and I found it extremely interesting.

Things at that time were not going well financially. One of my first jobs was to get rid of a recreational vehicle that he had. Not very long after that, the plane was gone. I didn't know Merrill well at that time. I had just met him, but there was nothing that said to me, "This is a man on the brink of financial failure." I never saw that in him. I never heard him say how awful it was or how affected he was. It was just, "Okay, it's time. We're going to have to do this; we're going to have to do that." I felt he managed it well.

Merrill didn't micromanage. He put guys like Rex Wilmore and Jerry Carlson in good spots and then left them alone. They were different from Merrill but very good at what they did. Jerry was the editor of Landowner at the time. It was his publication, and it would be his publication or he would not be there. Merrill recognized that. He identified closely with the journalists and would listen carefully to what they said. You got the impression that they were on an even par with him, but it was also apparent he was the boss.

I had been with Merrill two years, and he came to me one day and said, "Rex has another position, and I think you'd be well suited for it." I think he was truly looking out for me and knew there were other, perhaps bigger, things for me to do. Rex probably went through the biggest changes of all of the executives at Oster. He came into my office one day, I was sitting at my desk, and he plopped a computer in front of me. "Here," he said. "You need to learn how to use this," and gave me the instruction book. His life became very involved with technology and this was his way of dealing with it. We learned by doing.

Merrill was definitely a visionary. For example, when it came to Pinnacle Prairie where I now live, he saw the potential of what could happen out there whereas other people saw open land and two round barns.

I enjoyed working for Merrill. He was a demanding person. I think that entrepreneurs tend to be demanding, and that's part of why they succeed. If he asked you to do something, he expected you would do it, and do it correctly. I felt like he was definitely my boss, and yet he allowed me to feel that I was a responsible, capable, educated person.

Blasting through the Ownership Barrier
by Chris Crane

I met Merrill at a Campus Crusade for Christ event in the fall of '86. He told me he was looking to raise some financing and hired me as a consultant. I took him to several of my contracts on Wall Street, including several venture capitalists.

Merrill asked me to come to work for him full time. I became VP of Corporate Development and worked on finding financing and making acquisitions for Oster Inc. I saw up close that not only was Merrill a great entrepreneur, he was also a professional manager. That's a rare combination to have those two skill sets in one person. Merrill's faith was a shining light in my life. I worked under a very successful, dynamic Christian entrepreneur. He was a great example of a good business person who used his position to find opportunities to share Christ with others.

Once we obtained significant financing, my role was completed. I was offered a board position with a special project in San Diego, and Merrill gave me his blessing. He was already my mentor, and he agreed to continue as my mentor. He asked me to be on his advisory board, which I was happy to do. I learned a lot from the way he led those meetings and the way he drew advice from outsiders. I created my own advisory board when I was considering buying a company, and Merrill was on it. He was so helpful. I spent a weekend with him going through the upsides and the downsides and in the end he looked at me and said, "Chris, I see five things this company's doing wrong. If you fix these things, you can turn it around."

I bought the company and followed Merrill's advice. The company had lost money for five years in a row, which made it cheap to buy but also risky. I was putting up my life savings, and Merrill appreciated that. He's done that many times. He was very encouraging, and he took me through the negotiation process, then the turnaround process. He was a godsend for the whole endeavor.

My life would be so different had Merrill not asked me to join his company and mentor me through the acquisition of my own. And had he not given me those five strategic issues to correct, that company would not have made it. But it did and I was able to take the company public. That's what's given me the freedom to do ministry for the past 16 years.

Merrill's example of leadership has had such a big impact on me. He modeled being honest, trustworthy and kind but also being decisive and strong. He was loving and caring but also bold and courageous. I learned many things from Merrill that I've used as CEO of my own company and of Opportunity International.

He taught me never to surprise your bankers or your board. If you have a problem, let them know. He taught me to hire and retain only A players. A players are really good at what they do, who have a really good attitude and are a really good culture fit. If they don't have all three, they're not A players. Merrill would say, "A players hire other A players, and B players hire C players. B players don't want anyone as good or better than them." I used this lesson at Opportunity International, hiring good people, retaining them and encouraging them. His fingerprints are all over the success we had at Opportunity.

I've given up the CEO role now, but I still follow Merrill's example as a mentor. I've done a great deal of mentoring, and I love doing it.

At one point I wanted Merrill to shift from my advisory board to the regular board of my company, COMPS Info Systems. So did my venture capitalists because he had 25 years in the industry. But Merrill didn't do governance boards, so I needed something to attract him. "Look,

Merrill," I said. "When I sell the company, I'll donate one percent of the profits to Campus Crusade." He said, "I don't serve on boards, but your company might be valuable, and I don't know what I'd say to Dr. Bright if I don't do this." Once we went public and sold the company, it generated a large donation that Merrill used to fund Pinnacle Forum.

Merrill has been so pivotal. Without him I probably would've just taken a job somewhere and not have had the opportunities I've had. I can't say enough about him. He changed the trajectory of my life for the good.

CONSULTANT, PARTNER, FRIEND
by Steve James

I was an executive in different technology companies until 1993. I left the sector in a position to do what I wanted, so I started investing and consulting. I served on 18 boards over the years, and it was on the board of a company called COMPS that I met Merrill around 1994. COMPS's CEO was a mutual friend, Chris Crane.

Chris had led me to Christ in 1990, and I met Merrill about three years later. I refer to them as my spiritual bookends because the two of them really mentored me. They not only nurtured my growth as a Christian, they also showed me how to express my faith in the workplace. They had an enormous influence on my life.

After Merrill and I got to know each other, he asked me to help him sell his companies. He wanted to shift his time to ministry activities rather than business activity. In the process he wanted to turn his assets into liquidity so he could use them to serve the Lord. I found out that Merrill was a real entrepreneur and risk-taker. He did new things. When he started Pro Farmers, he was trying to level the playing field between farmers and the big grain companies. Farmers were good at planting and harvesting, but they didn't know a lot about the best ways to sell their crops or to hedge them in the process. Merrill was probably the first in the country to do that.

He did the same thing with brokers and dealers by publishing *Futures* magazine. Twenty years ago, if you walked into one of the big brokerage houses, there would be a *Futures* magazine sitting in their office. Then there was his company called Global Link. When the internet first became available via satellite, Merrill provided dishes and software to get online information to farmers in real time about grain prices. And there was a company called Future Source that aggregated about 50 data feeds from around the world into one data feed that he sold to individuals as well as traders at the big houses. Merrill was always doing something that hadn't been done before. He was a visionary.

Merrill was always pretty bold about his faith. That sometimes made me nervous because things had become much tighter about professing your faith in the marketplace. Especially when you're the CEO of a company. But Merrill was never intimidated by the restrictions of the law. He wouldn't make people uncomfortable, but he was happy to share the Good News with anybody he met. He was very bold about that. I got concerned from time to time because of potential litigation, but that never happened. The Lord protected him.

Merrill was in no hurry to sell his businesses, and the process took about 12 years. He wanted to do it in an orderly manner so as to maximize value. He delegated everything to me so he could focus on working with Bill Bright and with getting Pinnacle Forum off the ground.

The greatest guiding principles in Merrill's life come from the Bible. People talk about what's most important and they'll say God, family, and then country. Very few people live that out, but Merrill does. It's been very clear since the day I met him that his relationship with Jesus is more important than anything else. It's the driving force behind how he lives and makes his decisions. He's as astute and sophisticated as they come when it relates to business, but in many ways he's still a farm boy who lives by the Bible.

Merrill loves to hunt, and we've hunted together on one of his farms in Iowa he had designated as a bird preserve. He's taken groups from Pinnacle Forum and other nonprofits on hunts there. Once I with a group of about a dozen guys from Opportunity International. Chris Crane was the CEO at the time. A flush of about 20 birds got up all at once, and people started shooting. I'm shooting and turning, being careful, but not watching my feet. I stepped into a hole just as I shot and it knocked me backwards. I broke my right leg. After all the guns went off, birds were lying on the ground and so was I, moaning. Everyone thought I'd been shot.

I tell that story because in my office I have a pheasant I shot that Merrill had stuffed and mounted. It has a cast on its right leg. I've had a lot of fun with that guy.

MOVING A MISSION TO IOWA
by Dave Glock

I knew Merrill from speaking at his church in Waterloo. In time, he became a member of the Board of Trustees at Emmaus Bible College where I teach. We would meet on a regular basis from that point onward. He's a godly brother, very active in serving the Lord, and a great visionary, a big-picture man who has the gift of faith. He can trust God for some big things.

Merrill was heavily involved as a trustee in the move of the school from Oak Park, Illinois to Dubuque, Iowa, in the early '80s. He brought a great vision to the school. The two of us worked well together and established a pretty close relationship. It's difficult to get some people to move and it took his force, insight and vision to do that. The idea of, "Let's get the job done," was strong with Merrill. The thing that was so great about him was he not only said this, he really got involved in making it happen.

Merrill was a good speaker. He was good at anything public. He was, and still is, a student of Scripture. He was big on exhortation and vision. A visionary gives you a vision; that's what he does. He inspired a lot of people to get busy for God. He was always thinking ahead to what could be the next concentration of his energies, both spiritually and in the business world. He was just that kind of a person. He had definite opinions on how things should be done, but he presented them in a way that was acceptable. Anything new can be a real threat for more conservative folk. You have to bring them along to a consensus. He understood that. It took a few years, but it ultimately worked out very well.

Merrill contributed the use of his plane so we could get about quickly and maintain the day-by-day functioning of the school. We visited a number of places, and the one we finally decided to come down on was in Eastern Iowa. He gave us a lot of guidance in our selection. He worked not only on the idea but many of the mechanics of communicating the idea to our constituency in what we called the Vision '84 campaign. We flew all over the country putting on banquets, sharing the news, and he was behind a ton of that. He was a very active trustee during those years.

I always enjoyed Merrill's stretching other people to bigger and better ideas that were in keeping with the purposes and goals of the school. I doubt we'd be where we are today if he hadn't been involved with us, and that's a big statement. He had a lot to do with making a smooth transition between the Chicago area and Dubuque. He had big ideas, but he knew how to go about implementing them as well and how to work with the board. I've been at the school for 50 years and was the dean for 35 years. I've sat in on many board meetings. Merrill was one of the most influential of our trustees, to be sure.

PEERS IN BUSINESS, GOLF AND LIFE
by Larry Reed

Merrill's been a good friend of mine for a long time. I've known him since 1983. We are brothers in Christ, and we were in the Iowa chapter of Young Presidents' Organization together. We've both been company presidents and CEOs. I've been an entrepreneur just like him.

Within a few weeks of meeting him, Merrill gave me some videotapes of Dr. Bruce Wilkinson, Founder of Walk Through the Bible Ministries. Bruce was teaching the foundational courses for Fellowship of Companies for Christ International (FCCI). Merrill mentored me in applying biblical principles of management and leadership. The challenge issued by FCCI was "If God allows you to be president of a company, how will you use the platform he's given you to advance the gospel?"

One of the basic things they teach is pastoring your company, which was a novel idea to me at the time. This was my first encounter with servant leadership. Merrill modeled servant leadership in the marketplace. He's a hard-nosed entrepreneur, but he's also committed to Jesus Christ and he lives that out.

I actually remember one of our first breakfasts. It was July 3, 1983. Merrill's chin was on the table. He was an entrepreneur with dealings way beyond the means of most Iowa banks and the banks in Chicago were calling his loans. It was a tough blow, but God was at work. He seems to take entrepreneurs through tight squeeze in the marketplace from time to time. I had the privilege of walking beside Merrill and watching God bring him through. God used a group of FCCI leaders to help.

And there's a very close group of four guys who have prayed each other through some very difficult personal trials. We still play golf together. This year will be our 29th year in a row. Merrill and I have also done a lot of hunting together. I've been with the Pinnacle Forum guys who would come up to hunt on one of Merrill's farms. I was an Air Force flight instructor and enjoyed talking to Kenny Dahlberg and Joe Foss. I've got a great picture of Ken Lockard and Merrill and me and Joe in 1999.

I attended one of Campus Crusade for Christ President's Council meetings when Dr. Bright was launching History's Handful. Merrill was among his top leaders. Merrill not only gave a lot, but he helped raise a lot to advance the gospel around the world. I wasn't a "big hitter" back then, but now I've committed a lot of money to a ministry called Hope for India. Hope for India supports organizations that plant churches among some of the darkest areas on earth in North India. The reason for what I'm doing now goes back to the experience I had under Merrill's leadership and to watching Dr. Bright. That's why I'm taking the lead role in being a conduit of funds from myself and from the Charlotte real estate marketplace for this work.

Without Merrill's impetus in challenging and mentoring me, I don't know where I'd be. God's direction would have come from somewhere, but it came through Merrill and his example of servant leadership. He's visionary, he's a leader, he's not a common sort of a guy, especially in Iowa.

Merrill is one of thousands and thousands of Iowa farm boys, but he's the one out of those thousands to have achieved what he has achieved. He's comfortable on the Chicago Board of Trade and probably has deeper technical understanding of commodity markets and future markets than just about anybody. I remember being in his FutureSource office in Chicago. There aren't many Iowa guys in history who have offices in downtown Chicago. The next day we went to the

Chicago Athletic Club, and he let me sit in on a meeting with some lawyers. Again, there aren't very many Iowa guys who move in these circles.

What God has done through Merrill is phenomenal. His is a tremendous gospel story and entrepreneurial story. He's had a lot of influence in my life, for which I'm very thankful.

CHILDHOOD FRIENDS STICK TOGETHER
by Ron Kiewiet

Merrill and I were neighbor farm boys, and he was like a big brother to me. His mother was a second mother to me. I raised rabbits when I was a kid and got Merrill into raising rabbits. But I always had to go down and butcher his rabbits for him because I could do it faster. As teens we were involved in 4-H together. We showed our calves at the Butler County Fair. We would put a tarp over his dad's pickup, stuck a cooler full of food and sleep in the back of the pickup during the fair. I ran for the Butler county 4-H president, and I think it was because of a joke Merrill told about me that I was elected. He also helped me get a scholarship from Sears and Roebuck Foundation and got me to go to Iowa State rather than the University of Northern Iowa.

He was two years ahead of me, but we lived in the same house when I was a freshman. There were eight of us guys who lived upstairs two to a bedroom. I took over his photography business after he graduated. I also took over his job for the extension service on the radio with Dallas McGinnis.

After I graduated, I started selling mutual funds as a stockbroker. Merrill tried to get me to work for him, but I never did. I helped him a little but didn't do it for money. I was busy doing my own thing. We had adjoining offices when he first started in business in 1969. He just kept growing and ended up buying several building along Main Street. I was a one-man organization, and I've stayed a one-man organization. He's been very influential in our community. In addition to everything he's done downtown, he's got a big development called Pinnacle Prairie. I tease him by calling it Osterville, but he doesn't like that.

I knew Carol before she and Merrill got married. I went to country school with her. I thought they would be a good match. We attend the same church now, and Merrill was instrumental in getting me to go to Bethany.

Merrill and (his brother) Larry and I have gone hunting together since we were in grade school. Merrill's a good shot. Not as good as I am, but he's good. I've been on several of the hunts he sponsored on his farm. He always conducted himself with dignity and the utmost respect for everyone. He would lead us in prayer before the hunts. I met some very influential people from around the country. I really didn't know how influential some of these guys were. I'd never heard of Joe Foss for instance, but I looked him up afterwards and thought, wow.

Merrill has always been high caliber, always helpful, always very Christian. He led me to become a Christian. He has always expanded my horizons and pushed me to do better and achieve more, and he's helped me to do that my entire life. I have nothing but the highest regard for him.

Harnessing Merrill for Local Work
by Carolyn Hamrock

I recently retired from a long career in marketing, public relations and fund development. I have been very active in the Cedar Falls community. One of my first local projects was the restoration of what was then called the Regent Theatre. It is on First and Main Street at the gateway to the downtown area. It's on the same street as all of Merrill's offices at that time. Oster Communications was one of the major businesses in the area. It employed many people and was a strong economic force in the community.

I did a feasibility study on the viability of raising a few million dollars for the restoration and we started working actively together on this campaign. In the conclusion of the study, I recommended Merrill as the board chair, which he accepted. I found Merrill to be extremely dependable and hard working when he takes on a project. He is very visionary. I was impressed with all of the effort he put into Restore the Regent, including giving the capstone gift of $140,000.

The theatre was more than 100 years old, and Merrill's efforts were a critical piece in keeping it from being turned into a parking lot. Now it is fittingly called the Oster Regent Theatre. It has added economic value to the community and is a resource for children and adults who take different lessons there. Working together was a wonderful experience. I just cannot give Merrill enough accolades for our success.

Later I got involved with some of the clients at a development of Merrill's called Pinnacle Prairie. It's another example of his vision for our community. It started with Merrill's farmland and has been his baby to grow. It's still being developed with churches, a retirement home, stores, businesses and banks. It's a project you don't develop in a couple of years. It's great for Cedar Falls, and City Hall is happy because of the tax dollars coming from there.

Merrill has also been involved in projects nationwide, particularly with nonprofits and ministries. Our paths crossed again in the early 1990s with Campus Crusades' *Jesus* Film Project. I helped them put together their strategic plan and recommended Merrill as one of 20 business people to be on their national advisory board. He accepted and I had the opportunity to see him at a few meetings. He provided a strong endorsing vision to the plan to raise millions of dollars for the gospel.

And when Merrill was starting Pinnacle Forum, I was asked for some ideas to jumpstart the ministry. I didn't work contractually with them but became a volunteer resource because I believed in what Merrill was doing. His heart and soul have been in Pinnacle Forum, and Carol's too.

Carol chose to be more in the background, as she was with Restore the Regent campaign. She attended the events and functions, and all that goes along with being major donors. She's a wonderful person and very supportive of Merrill, but she's more comfortable having Merrill in front and being a support for him.

Merrill and Carol have had a great impact in my life and that of my husband, Jim. They are people of strong faith, which is one of the things I admire about them.

From Pinnacle Peak to Pinnacle Forum
by Bill Dodder

I was with Campus Crusade, and I went to Phoenix to work on the vision Dr. Bright called The One Percent Strategy. I started meeting with the top 1 percent of influencers. I had met Merrill at some Crusade events around the country. He would winter in the area, and we started running together. Then we started a Bible study at The Boulders Golf Club.

We wound up living just a few blocks apart in Terravita. We played golf and ran every morning and we discussed stuff like The One Percent Strategy. Right after that Dr. Bright recruited Merrill for the effort. I introduced Merrill to Terry Hamlin who had come down with me from Colorado to work on the *Jesus* film project. I think we had about 100 or so churches involved.

One day Merrill and Terry and I went hiking on Pinnacle Peak, and we talked about all of this and prayed for the whole town. As we were coming down, Merrill suggested the name Pinnacle Forum. We were at Pinnacle Peak and he was involved with Forum groups, so he tied the two together and named the thing Pinnacle Forum.

Later, we were at a friend of mine's house in Beaver Creek, Colorado, where we actually launched Pinnacle Forum. We did a Super Bowl breakfast for about 1,000 people and started a lot of Bible studies with some really high-powered guys. More than anybody else, Merrill was the financing behind Pinnacle Forum. Other guys gave, but nothing compared to what Merrill did.

I was impressed by Merrill's commitment to personal evangelism and his positive energy. He got a membership at a new golf course and bought me a membership. We used golf as a tool for evangelism. The first thing we did was pray on the first hole. That set the tone for talking to these guys for the next four hours.

We lived for evangelism and Pinnacle Forum. There were lots of 16-hour days and Merrill had an unlimited amount of energy. I don't know if you can wear him out. We ran six days a week. We ran marathons, but Merrill did a lot more of them than me. We went down the Grand Canyon a few times with Frank Toney. He mentored guys like Frank and took them under his wing.

At one point Merrill wanted me to take over things with Pinnacle Forum, but I don't have the organization skills. I'm not that kind of guy. I left Crusade and returned to Colorado in 2000. I started several Forum-type groups. I also started three churches in Colorado Springs and lots of Bible studies, something I've done all my life.

The time with Merrill and Terry and a handful of guys was a unique time of God's anointing. I was blessed like I've never been blessed before. Merrill was a big part of that with his unlimited energy for evangelism and incredible passion for giving.

ACCELERATING MINISTRIES IS OUR REAL WORK
by Ken Lockard

My history with Merrill and Carol is very deep and rich. We went to the same church. Our families have been intricately woven. Carol was my babysitter when I was a kid. Her parents and my parents were best of friends. Carol is a prayer warrior, and Merrill is the leader. She follows along and is the pray-er behind the man who really makes things happen.

Merrill is very generous and uses everything he owns for the cause of Christ. He's had Pinnacle Forum and a number of other ministries out to his farms to hunt. At these events he's introduced me to some of the neatest people I've ever known. The camaraderie and the fellowship and fun we had in those times. People's lives were changed out in those cornfields because he was willing to organize a bunch of events and bring men together. He probably did that for 25 years.

Merrill just loves bringing people to Christ. I've never met a guy quite like him who is unafraid of sharing the Gospel. It doesn't matter who he's talking to. Honestly, it could be the president of the United States. When my sister was getting married, Merrill got with her fiancé and led him to the Lord. This was probably five years ago. Merrill has discipled him on a weekly basis from then until today. Wherever Merrill is, he will get on the phone, and they will have an hour together of Bible study and prayer.

He is unafraid to cast big visions; then he finds talented people to help make them happen. It doesn't matter if it's in Pinnacle Forum or his business. Merrill had his old office in downtown Cedar Falls and he became the president of the Cedar Falls Chamber of Commerce. At that time, two-thirds of the downtown was empty. Merrill started an initiative to fill up the spaces and clean up everything. He pulled the right people around him, and he also made sure that he had the right next three presidents coming in behind him who would fulfill the vision he had cast. Since then downtown Cedar Falls has been voted Best Little Downtown in the United States several times. It all came from Merrill's vision way back when.

I'm one of the many guys Merrill has mentored. He is an open book when it comes to his own life. I mean, he's had some tragedies, and by sharing them with me, someone who is 15 years younger, he has helped me not trip over a number of different hurdles or make the same mistakes.

Merrill really helped me clarify my vision for serving Christ. I have a heart for CEOs. They create a pretty broad swathe when it comes to culture change within their organizations. I think they are the loneliest people in the world and they have no one to talk to. I've had the opportunity to be involved with bringing many CEOs to Christ.

I've met many of them through organizations like YPO and Pinnacle Forum. Merrill got me involved with both. I remember he came into the office one day and said, "Look, you're a young president, and you need to be in YPO." I said, "What is YPO?" He told me all about it and he said, "I'm going down next week." So I go to YPO for my first time, and they're setting up new forums. Before I was even a member in YPO, Merrill got me into a forum.

He was after me for years to get involved with Pinnacle Forum. For some reason, I just couldn't see the vision. Then he got me to meet with their board, and I just fell in love with those guys. I ended up starting four Forum groups here in the Cedar Valley. I even served 11 years on the National Pinnacle Forum Board. YPO and Pinnacle Forum are really two of the incredible catalysts in my life on the business side and the spiritual side.

Merrill is an incredible encourager. He would never say, You should be doing this. Instead, he would make suggestions or talk about other people and what they were doing so you could see that opportunity in your own life. Because of him I've served on multiple boards including the board of Vision 360, whose mission is to plant 50 churches in the 500 largest cities in the world.

Merrill can have a hard edge, and people can take offense at that. What people will find out is that after he's given a karate chop, if you will, if they will give him the opportunity to express what he's thinking, they'll come away feeling much better. Behind the hard edge, he has a spiritual tenderness.

Sometimes I don't even know how he does it; he just gets amazing things done. Other than my father, Merrill has meant more to me than any man, and I love him dearly. I think so highly of him that I want him to be proud of me and pay it forward.

Serving Church and Community Together
by Bob Smith Jr.

Merrill's had a huge impact in my life. He and my dad were elders together at Downing Avenue Gospel Chapel, now Bethany Bible Chapel. I grew up respecting him as a leader, as someone whom my dad respected and had a close friendship with. My own church involvement has been inspired by these men. I got married young, and my wife and I worked with high school kids for about 18 years at Downing Avenue Gospel Chapel and now Bethany. We've also hosted a young men's Bible study. We've sought to follow their example of investing in specific lives.

As a young person, I worked at Merrill's company in the summers before going off to college. After that, I started my own business and stayed in touch with him. I now work with Lockard Companies. In 2004 Merrill engaged us as a master developer to help carry out his vision for Pinnacle Prairie in Cedar Falls. It's a 700-acre master planned community. He bought the ground over a few decades and wanted to give back to his hometown by doing some quality development that smaller developments aren't able to do.

I've been able to work with Merrill from then until now. I was a young executive just building a team. Having him as both a mentor and a client was very good for us. One of the skills he taught me was to bring in the best people for each specific area and to use their expertise to make a project the best it can be. Instead of trying to do everything yourself, find people who are great at what they do and incorporate them into what you're creating. The genius of that permeates a lot of what I do today as a business professional.

Merrill has also had a big impact on my partner, Ken Lockard. Merrill invited Ken into the Young Presidents' Organization, and Ken, in turn, got me invited into YPO, which has made a big impression on me. A lot of things that originated with Merrill have been passed on to a number of folks who are a generation or half generation ahead of where I am. His thinking and passion are being multiplied through those he's influenced and have had a compound effect on me. I'm also in a Pinnacle Forum, an organization he started.

One of the people Merrill introduced me to is Steve James. Steve has helped with the business and as a mentor. So has Chris Crane, a guy Merrill mentored who has taken an interest in me. Merrill and Steve and Chris have not only impacted my life but they have had an impact on my son Levi as well. The first time we went to Mexico with Steve to build houses, Levi was only six. We've been a few times since.

Merrill used to put on some big hunts at his farm as fundraisers for ministries. I would bring Levi as a six-, seven-, eight-year-old, and he always looked forward to being in the van with Mr. Oster. My son is 22 now, and if he has a deep question, Merrill is one of the people he will talk to. Whether Merrill's at the front of starting Pinnacle Forum or in a farm field with a kid, he sees the value of each person to the Lord and he values them himself.

Merrill has challenged me in the way he's very bold about who he is in Christ. He's not pushy, but he lets people know his grounding is in Jesus Christ. He doesn't miss many opportunities to communicate the difference Christ has made in this life. I remember talking with Merrill once about how to give to the Lord's work. He said, "Bob, if God chooses to entrust you with financial means, you need to be a wise steward of those funds." When I asked how to do that, he said, "After giving to your church first, look at your other giving as somewhat similar to a stock portfolio. Some giving may be low or no risk, and then you may have some you take a chance on. Trust the Lord to accomplish what he needs to with the funds he's entrusted to you."

Merrill has consistently been someone who's committed to God, to family and to people. He works hard at finding better ways of doing things. He's never settled for mediocre; he's always pushed for the best. He's not perfect, but he's always been kind and generous. I'm so thankful he's in my life.

Mentors for Life
by Tim O'Conner

My connection with Merrill is an offshoot of all that happened before me. I was just the beneficiary of all those years of strong relationship with the Lockard family. Merrill and my late father-in-law, Wendell Lockard, were best friends. I met Merrill in April 2011 when I was getting married to January Lockard. I'd heard so many stories about him and had this strong urge to meet him, so I gave him a call and said, "I'm getting this feeling we need to meet before the wedding."

We had breakfast the next morning and a really good conversation that quickly made a sharp turn toward where I stood spiritually. Not being a Christian at the time, I didn't have a whole lot to say, and it was that morning that Merrill led me to the Lord.

Since that first breakfast, Merrill and I have been getting together every Friday morning. When our schedules permit, we meet face to face. When he's elsewhere, we get together on the phone. We spend an hour in Bible study or go through different books. We keep it all Bible based. We try to find new ways to grow as men, as husbands, as friends, as sons and brothers, but also to find ways to have a positive effect on our communities.

I've been walking outside while doing a Bible study with Merrill, carrying my book and FaceTiming him. He may be in his car or in a duck blind. He could be anywhere. We just find a way to make it work. It's a very special part of our lives. I don't think he realized what a big project he would have when we got started but he's hanging in there with me.

I remember right after I got married, I was laid off for four months. Merrill and I kept praying and talking about it. He helped me to hang in there and get through it. I learned to put my faith in the Lord and trust God.

He's been very open about his own life. Every time things are getting tight businesswise, we just pray about it, and somehow, he just keeps plugging along. That's one of the lessons he's taught me. No matter what happens, you have to keep praying and thanking the Lord and trusting that it's in God's plan. If you can keep that perspective, all the little things don't matter as much.

Merrill's a tremendous friend and a tremendous influence. But it's much more than a friendship. There's so many different angles that he's brought to our relationship. It isn't just a mentoring situation; it's so much more. It's like the love of a father and a friend who cares about you, but he's also a working professional who gives me guidance with my career.

I've golfed with Merrill, and one of the unique things about him is no matter who he's with, before he tees off, he always finds a way to bring everybody together and say a quick prayer. That's not easy to do with a bunch of guys who just want to play golf and have fun and who aren't Christians. But he always has a way of doing it where he makes people feel comfortable.

It's a lifelong commitment when you become friends with Merrill because no matter how bad you screw up, he always forgives you and continues to be as Christlike as he can, which has an impact on those of us who are lucky enough to be associated with him. I have a lot closer relationship with Merrill than I've ever had with my own father or brothers or any other friend, for that matter.

I'm not even close to being the kind of mentor Merrill is, but I've certainly learned a lot from him. I've tried to use those things he shared with my stepsons and our daughter's fiancé.

I don't know where I'd be today without Merrill's mentoring. He's been such a special man to me. I would be absolutely lost had he not extended his time and his wisdom and his knowledge and his love to me.

Preventing a Train Wreck While Preaching the Gospel
by Gene Redlin

When I came on board, Commodity Communications Corp. (later FutureSource) in Lombard, Illinois, the company was in a fairly distressed situation. There were a lot of practices that weren't appropriate for the size company it was. The first thing I did was focus on getting the company to stop bleeding money. It was exciting to aggressively find ways to stop the bleeding and turn it around. When I came, we were losing $50,000 a month, and by the time I left, it was making $50,000 a month. That's a pretty good-sized turnaround.

My management style was somewhat more authoritarian than Merrill's. His style was more collaborative. Under the circumstances the company required a pretty strong hand, and I provided that. Merrill never second-guessed my operational style. He knew when he hired me that he needed results. He needed somebody to turn things around. I'm not much driven by approval. Merrill wasn't either. He never needed somebody to pat him on the back all the time. He didn't require anybody to kiss up to him, which I appreciated.

I enjoyed Merrill, and he seemed to think I was okay. We had a lot of shared values. Both of us came from a rich Christian heritage. I felt he understood what it meant to be a believer and to be a good businessman at the same time. It was a positive motivation in me coming to work for him.

We didn't have a formalized mentoring environment, but we did a lot of training. I think it's impossible to be in any business, or in life for that matter, where you're not constantly being formed. Mentoring takes place because we're shaped by our experiences and our interactions with other people.

I was there from the fall of '85 through '90 when the

decision was made to modify the management team and bring in another CEO. It appeared to me that my style of management no longer fit. The parting was amiable. I wasn't angry or particularly upset. I understood Merrill's focus was different from mine at that time. I could appreciate the developments going on. Rex Wilmore and Mike Rodby were taking the company in a positive direction.

I am very thankful for the opportunity to develop some skill sets I did not have walking into FutureSource. Merrill gave me the chance to find my way. I took advantage of the assets we had like John Schillaci, our CFO at that time. I bent his ear a lot and learned a lot from him.

Another benefit, the big one, was that Merrill let me explore every kind of potential for marketing and positioning, even globally. I spent time in Japan, Taiwan, Brazil and Europe. I also worked in Florida, California and New York to deepen the marketing side of the company. I don't think I would have been afforded such free reign anywhere else. Merrill trusted me to do what was right and I believe I served him well.

I knew some of Merrill's background, how his dad's passing had affected him. I think mortality is something that as Christians we have to recognize. We're not moribund about that, but it's important to consider. There's more to life than business. When I was with Merrill a few years ago, he talked about his family and his joy at being able to be part of their lives. I feel the same way about my own children.

After Merrill started Pinnacle Forum, he invited me to a group. I visited but it wasn't a fit for me at that point. Instead I've been involved with CBMC and businessmen's roundtable type groups. I believe it's very important for Christian men to have fellowship with other Christian men and be able to sound off with each other. I've also helped start a couple of churches here in St. Charles, Illinois.

I'm still using what I learned at FutureSource. I'm actively engaged in doing financial forensics for corporations all over the country. It's really quite rewarding. Merrill helped me be where I am today in my ability to manage at a higher level than I ever could have had I stayed in North Dakota.

FORUM CONNECTION
by Bruce Everette

Pinnacle Forum, of which Merrill is a founder, plays a big role in my life. I'm chair of the national board and I'm on the Arizona board for Pinnacle Forum. I facilitate several different Forums and do some individual leadership coaching. I'm financially supporting and involved with a few ministries I would not have known about if not for Pinnacle Forum such as Christian Family Care, Phoenix Rescue Mission and Choices Pregnancy Centers.

I met Merrill at my first board meeting. I'd been introduced to Pinnacle Forum after I retired. I got to know Merrill better as we had coffee a few times. As a founder of Pinnacle Forum, he might be perceived by people who don't know him as being rigid in the way he thinks it should be run and not open to new ideas. But I found him to be just the opposite.

Merrill wants to know what other people think. He listens with an open mind and heart. He's very open to new things. For example, we were having difficulty growing until somebody introduced us to Zoom technology and the video forum concept. There was lots of resistance at first. People were saying you can't build relationships like this. It's not going to work. But this past year, most of our growth can be attributed to video forums. They make it easy for Partners to attend. Business people who are traveling can be anywhere in the country and sign on. I've signed on to them everywhere from Hawaii to Washington DC.

Merrill is one of the biggest supporters of video forums because they get people involved. They are making a difference in people's lives and influencing individuals who in turn influence the culture. He takes time with individuals. Although he's made a big impact collectively, he concentrates on impacting individuals and then the impact they have on others. That's basically what Pinnacle Forum does.

I wish the Forum experience had been available to me 25 years ago. In the position I was in as an executive, I couldn't talk to competitors. I was on the board for an organization that brought all the presidents of local food chains together, but we always had an attorney present and could only talk about certain things. And I couldn't talk to people within the company. I couldn't confide personal stuff to colleagues at the office because it would ultimately be used against me. At the same time, it would have been very difficult for me to be in a regular Forum group because I traveled 80 percent of the time. I didn't have a consistent schedule where I could have been there. But with video forums, I could have participated no matter where I was.

When I did start attending a Forum group, we had a couple guys who were really struggling in their marriages. They felt comfortable in sharing what was going on, and we'd pray for them. As I listened to these gentlemen talk about the difficulties they were having, it made me realize how blessed I was with the woman God had put in my life. It gave me a whole new appreciation for my wife. It also made me a better listener to her and my two daughters.

In addition to my Forum involvement, I've served on some volunteer boards like Easter Seals, American Heart Association and City of Hope. I'm an elder at my church, and I've shared with Merrill about it. He's given me some good guidance on that front. I know he prays for me, and that's been great.

I tell people that Merrill is the type of person I want to grow up to be like. I'm not far behind Merrill as far as age goes. I have a lot of respect for him, and I admire what he's done.

Life Tips

One
Farm Boy

Life tip #1: Stand on the Word of God.

Life tip #2: Put God first.

Life tip #3: Love one another by investing quality time.

Life tip #4: Get a life—a spiritual one.

Life tip #5: Protect your reputation.

Life tip #6: Bad decisions have bad consequences.

Life tip #7: Pace yourself.

Life tip #8: Have a plan.

Life tip #9: Set priorities.

Life tip #10: Start with sweat equity.

Life tip #11: Create wealth by earning it.

Life tip #12: Learn to manage complexity.

Life tip #13: Mix in a little fun.

Life tip #14: Buy land. Own your farm.

Life tip #15: Get an eternal perspective.

Life tip #16: Memorize Bible verses; you'll need them.

Life tip #17: Move beyond knowledge to belief.

Life tip #18: Tell others what God has done for you.

Two
Early Education
Life tip #19: Embrace change or get buried.
Life tip #20: If at first you don't succeed, try again.
Life tip #21: Pick your fights carefully.
Life tip #22: Be prepared before you step on the platform.
Life tip #23: Be a lifelong learner.
Life tip #24: You can change your world—speak up!
Life tip #25: Follow your inner guide—the Holy Spirit.
Life tip #26: Develop discipline.
Life tip #27: Become frugal.
Life tip #28: Make informed decisions.
Life tip #29: Set goals and reward service.
Life tip #30: Let the words of your elders settle in your soul.

Three
Solid Foundation
Life tip #31: Find a good mentor and listen.
Life tip #32: God speaks, sometimes in a crisis.
Life tip #33: Dream big, but get a job.
Life tip #34: Let your action follow your prayer.
Life tip #35: When you find her, never let her go.
Life tip #36: Know the lifetime value of a customer.
Life tip #37: Study to grow spiritually.
Life tip #38: Learn from the best.
Life tip #39: Just get to the nub of the story.
Life tip #40: Know the top 1 percent.
Life tip #41: Serve your church and community.
Life tip #42: Keep your options open.
Life tip #43: Take pie when pie is passed.
Life tip #44: Take a career assessment break.
Life tip #45: Validate your answers to prayer, then act.
Life tip #46: Never sell yourself too cheaply.

Four
Professional Farmers of America
Life tip #47: Start with a big, unique idea.

Life tip #48: Test your big idea.

Life tip #49: Attract the best talent available.

Life tip #50: Don't be afraid of risk.

Life tip #51: Exceed your clients' expectations.

Life tip #52: Build a strong team.

Life tip #53: Deliver a unique message.

Life tip #54: Get insights from your peers.

Life tip #55: Test, test, test!

Life tip #56: Pay up for the best advice.

Life tip #57: Shared values create a strong culture.

Life tip #58: Expect unique contributions.

Life tip #59: We need each other.

Five
Buying, Selling, Building Equity
Life tip #60: Take only risks you can afford.

Life tip #61: Manage your risk with futures.

Life tip #62: Always be ready to buy or sell.

Life tip #63: Cut your losses short.

Life tip #64: Use leverage wisely.

Six
Futures Magazine, FutureSource, Oster Dow Jones
Life tip #65: Leverage sales by cross selling.

Life tip #66: Trust but verify.

Life tip #67: Hire the right person at the right time.

Life tip #68: Hire and cultivate unique skills.

Life tip #69: Admit mistakes, ask forgiveness.

Life tip #70: Prayer and fellowship lighten burdens.

Life tip #71: Listen to the voice of the marketplace.

Life tip #72: The second half need not be a repeat.

Seven
Cedar Falls
Life tip #73: Leading by giving pays dividends.
Life tip #74: There is joy in serving others.

Eight
Family First
Life tip #75: Count your blessing in times of crisis.
Life tip #76: Get multiple second opinions.
Life tip #77: Thank God daily for good health.

Nine
Pinnacle Forum America
Life tip #78: Share your faith to change the world.
Life tip #79: Some yearn for Christ. They need your help.
Life tip #80: Trials prepare us for the next assignment.
Life tip #81: A few influencers can change cultures.
Life tip #82: We can accelerate someone else's passion.
Life tip #83: There is a time to lead and a time to follow.
Life tip #84: Spiritual exercise leads to cultural change.
Life tip #85: Passionate leaders can make a big difference.
Life tip #86: Influence future generations now.

Ten
Spiritual Fitness
Life tip #87: Don't give up your dreams.
Life tip #88: Build a strong team of advisors.
Life tip #89: Spiritual fitness produces goal achievement.
Life tip #90: Leave footprints for others to follow.

Eleven
Harvest Time
Life tip #91: Time investments are as important as money
investments.
Life tip #92: Set expectations by God's standards.

Influential Books and Authors

God has used book authors to shape me. Authors tend to inform and influence my thinking at strategic times when I find a book that fits the need in the moment. I'm an avid reader, and many of my mentors have been authors who interpreted biblical principles so I could apply them in my own life. Rather than mention these titles in their historical context, I've collected them here, in no particular order.

Your Work Matters to God by Doug Sherman and William Hendricks put meat on the bone Grandma Carrie gave me when she said, "God owns it all. All you do is for him. Use your car, your job, hour hobbies, everything as a way to tell others about Jesus." I began to see work as part of my worship after reading this book. These authors helped me understand that the Great Commission directive to make disciples goes beyond leading people to a saving faith, but is more of one in which the mentor teaches a lifestyle of service to others and obedience to God.

Stanley Tam's *God Is My Copilot* hit my desk in my twenties and gave me backbone to speak out for Christ in public. Max DePree, whom I never met, gave me additional backbone to use my companies as a platform for Christian service and witness.

I was introduced to C. S. Lewis through a friend giving me a copy of *Mere Christianity* about the time we launched *Pro Farmer* in 1973. His powerful argument that one must acknowledge Jesus Christ as liar, lunatic or Lord provided a great framework for future conversations with people I talked with who said Jesus was just a very good man. That's an intellectual inconsistency given that Jesus Christ claimed to be God. Insights like this made for intelligent conversation with my skeptic friends, and I met a lot of them in the commodity futures industry.

I read hundreds of business books because my degrees were in journalism. I had to learn how to run companies on the fly. Books that were helpful in our high-growth era were *Built to Last* by James Collins and *In Search of Excellence* by Tom Peters and Robert Waterman. Always searching to hear from the best, I attended seminars held by these authors and must give them credit for giving me the courage to move people around or fire them when we had the "wrong people in the right chair" or were doing the "wrong thing at the right time." The team building ideas in these books laid the base for our teaching team building in our companies, primarily by hiring outside consultants to deliver the message to "lead, follow or get out of the way."

Power for Living by Jamie Buckingham impressed me with how Arthur DeMoss through his foundation could impact our culture by advertising this book in newspapers. The book influenced my own presentations of the gospel, both in my writings and in speeches. *Born Again* by Billy Graham had a similar influence on my presentations. Keep it simple!

Christian Basics by John Scott and *Kingdom Living* by John MacArthur have provided some mental framework for presentations. *The Wonderful Spirit-Filled Life* and other books by Charles Stanley including the *30 Life Principles*

Bible have been of great encouragement to me and men I have mentored.

Hudson Taylor's Spiritual Secret by Howard and Geraldine Taylor, and *The Spiritual Man* by Watchman Nee gave me the picture of truly godly men, totally committed to the Lord. Here I saw the great potential for further growth in my own life by using these men as models. I was not then, and am still not, in their league spiritually!

Fellow Christian in the futures industry, Grant Noble, author of *The Trader's Edge* encouraged me by its inscription inside the front cover: "To Merrill Oster, a true Christian witness in a very pagan industry." His book, like Conrad Leslie's book *Successful Commodity Trading* had tips that I incorporated into my futures trading, an activity in which I engaged in profitably but one in which I encourage my friends to avoid.

There's an inscription, one from Leo Melamed, in *Escape to the Futures*: "You were there at the beginning and helped shape the destiny of futures." That is particularly meaningful because Leo, as president of the Chicago Mercantile Exchange, brought trading in currencies and treasuries and other contracts into existence and propelled the industry into a period of incredible growth. He knew me as president of Professional Farmers of America, which encouraged 30,000 farmers to use futures to manage risk, and as publisher of *Futures* magazine, the voice of the futures industry with 65,000 subscribers.

Books by fellow Christian businessmen have been particularly helpful. Bill Pollard, whom I met as a fellow board member at Emmaus College, wrote *Serving Two Masters* and *Soul of the Firm.* My personal visits with Bill gave me the backbone to state in my own company purpose that which guided his ServiceMaster company. Purpose: to serve God.

Over the years I have given away a few hundred copies of *Bringing Out the Best in People* by Alan Loy McGinnis. His ideas on relationship building made this a hand out to every business associate. His theme: learn to enjoy helping others excel.

My copy of *The Pursuit of the Holy* by J. Oswald Sanders is falling apart through overuse. It is marked up, highlighted and dog-eared. Sanders has led me back to a deeper presence of God after periods of business seemingly crowded God out. He reminded me during trials that, "No trial or affliction can reach those who are abiding in Him without His permission."

In an age when some influencers make wealth seem dirty, Brian Griffiths in *The Creation of Wealth* taught me how to think about wealth creation as the solution to poverty, the opportunity to invest in job creation and a way to give back.

Bruce Wilkenson's personal ministry to me through seminars has been a big part of my spiritual development. His books *The Prayer of Jabez* and *Secrets of the Vine* caught me at just the right time. I was praying the prayer of Jabez on a day of prayer and fasting in the desert with Frank Toney when God nudged me to realize my borders needed no further expansion—better cultivate what you have. Bruce stimulated the meditation process that led to a major downsizing of my financial exposure in the 1990s.

I served on the Here's Life Publishing board with Ted Engstrom. Bob Owen wrote his biography in *Ted Engstrom: Man with a Vision*. Ted's own book, *The Making of a Christian Leader*, was meaningful because I could see the manuscript lived out in real life by serving with him. Ted's humble, yet powerful way of expressing God's love impacted the Youth for Christ movement, World Vision and Zondervan Publishing and influenced the way I thought about using my own influence. Ted was a model, both in person and in print.

Bob Buford, author of *Halftime*, served on the Oster advisory board and helped me think about starting a second career in volunteer service and organization-building while running several for profit companies. He introduced me to one of my favorite business authors, his friend Peter Drucker. I sat almost spellbound at a meeting Bob put together for a dozen of his friends, billed as "an evening with Peter Drucker." Drucker's *Managing the Nonprofit Organization* and *Managing in Turbulent Times* were just what I needed in navigating the crises in the 1980s and 1990s, then making the transition into nonprofit work.

Celebration of Discipline by Richard Foster and *Spirit of the Disciplines* by Dallas Willard influenced my thinking while preparing for my doctoral studies. I came to the conclusion that, although faith alone secures our eternal destiny, it is through the spiritual fitness exercises such as prayer, fellowship, giving, service, solitude and worship that we develop spiritual muscle. And, it is the formation of spiritual muscle that paves the way for personal and cultural transformation.

John C. Maxwell's *Becoming a Person of Influence* gave me a view of leadership at its highest level, developing leadership skills in others. This book hit my lap as we were developing the first roll out of Pinnacle Forum nationally. I saw my role clearly as a coach and influencer of men and women who were already leaders in their own spheres. My role was one of challenging them to join a Pinnacle Forum to see how God would move them from beyond earthly success to making an eternal impact.

Lifeviews by R. C. Sproul and *Business* by Wayne Grudem helped me shape my thinking on how Pinnacle Forum can help its Partners see that the Bible must be the filter through which we attempt to impact our culture.

Somehow books like *Think and Grow Rich* by Napoleon

Hill have found their way into my mind and library. Hill's idea of forming a "brain trust" of some of the best people you can find seeped into my thinking. A Young Presidents' Organization's forum or Pinnacle Forum achieves a similar purpose by finding fellow sojourners who bounce life decisions off each other. Brain trusts are a vital source of direction and energy in my life. Thanks, Mr. Hill!

When it comes to books other than the Bible that have drawn me closer to the Lord, *Knowing God* by J. I. Packer and *To Be Near unto God* by Abraham Kuyper top the list. And as far as techniques to get me closer, reading Bill Bright's *How to Be Filled with the Holy Spirit* and *First Love* and using daily devotionals like *My Utmost for His Highest* by Oswald Chambers have given me some precious moments.

I am influenced daily by resources such as Dave Jeremiah's *Turning Points* opened at the breakfast table. Rick Warren's *Purpose Driven Life* daily emails and Guy Rodger's podcasts form Pinnacle Forum keep me encouraged and directed. I read a book or two a month, not counting those I travel thorough with my fellow Pinnacle Forum Partners.

Made in the USA
Columbia, SC
05 April 2019